Never Been Here Before?

a genealogists' guide to the Family Records Centre

Jane Cox
and
Stella Colwell

Genealogy is the perfect hobby

Peace perfect peace
With loved ones far away.

From the hymn by Bishop Bickersteth who had sixteen children.

Acknowledgements

The authors would like to thank the staff at the Family Records Centre for their help, in particular Foluke Abiona, Ruth Edwards, Karen Grannum, Joan Burr and Mona Singh. Thanks also go to Jill Eckersley, Anna Taylor and Gerry Hames of the Office for National Statistics, Millie Skinns, Marion Edwards, Melvyn Stainton and Julia Wigg of PRO Publications, Norah Conrad for permission to use her family tree and Trevor Chalmers for the drawings.

The birth, marriage and death certificates that appear in the book were obtained from the Office for National Statistics. The design of the certificates is Crown copyright, and is reproduced with the permission of the Controller of HMSO.

PRO Publications
Public Record Office
Ruskin Avenue
Kew
Richmond
Surrey
TW9 4DU
http://www.pro.gov.uk/

© Crown Copyright 1997; 3rd printing 1998

ISBN 1 873162 41 3

A catalogue card for this book
is available from the British Library.

CONTENTS

ILLUSTRATIONS

Where to find the Family Records Centre

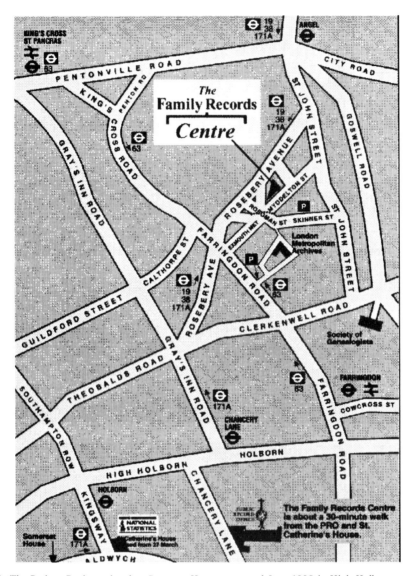

NB: The Probate Registry closed at Somerset House; reopened June 1998 in High Holborn

Family Records Centre, 1 Myddelton Street, London EC1R 1UW.
Telephone: certificate enquires - 0151 471 4800; other enquiries - 0181 392 5300.

Opening hours: Monday, Wednesday and Friday 9 am to 5 pm
Tuesday 10 am to 7 pm
Thursday 9 am to 7 pm
Saturday 9.30 am to 5 pm (except for some Saturdays preceding
    Easter and Christmas; please check before you visit)
Closed Sundays and Bank Holidays.

PART I
Introduction

ABOUT THIS BOOK

This guide is intended to provide anyone who has literally 'Never Been Here Before' with an informal, but informed, introduction to the new Family Records Centre at Myddelton Street in London. The Family Records Centre, which is run jointly by the Office for National Statistics and the Public Record Office, brings together for the first time under one roof some of the most important sources and indexes used by family historians. This book offers you detailed practical advice as to how the system works in both parts of the Centre and explains how to begin your research. Inter-related entries from registers of births, marriages and deaths, census returns, wills and other public records show exactly what the records will tell you and how your family tree can be put together.

A companion volume, *New to Kew?* by Jane Cox, has already been published to introduce readers to the most important genealogical sources housed in the Public Record Office at Kew. A new edition of the in-depth handbook, *Tracing Your Ancestors in the Public Record Office*, will be published in late 1998.

Researching your family history - the perfect hobby

Family History is now one of the most popular hobbies in this country. In the last three decades what was once called 'genealogy', the pursuit of pedigrees, has changed into 'Family History'. The old discipline, which was largely confined to the wealthy, leisured classes, tended to concern itself solely with the search for a line (paternal) stretching back as far as may be. Family History takes in as many twigs and branches as it can, spreading its arms wide along all the lines available for research. Not only does it encourage 'sideways growth', it looks into the lives and preoccupations of our ancestors, putting them into their proper historical context. Any ordinary person can have their own personal slice of history.

In the past genealogy involved a good deal of travelling round the country in search of records, digging around in dingy church vestries and traipsing through churchyards. These days it is very different and the recently opened Family Records Centre has made research infinitely more straightforward than it was hitherto, bringing together under one roof access to the prime sources for England and Wales (and some for Scotland, too) going back several hundred years.

Armed with nothing more than your own place and date of birth (if it was in England or Wales) you may be able to get your family back as far as the eighteenth century or even to Tudor times without having to go to any other archive or library.

No specialist knowledge is required to start, although you will acquire skills in reading old handwriting as you go along and be inspired to inform yourself about the past in the wider context.

Before you start, there are a few things you should think about...

Has anyone traced my family before?

First, as it says in all the Family History guide books, ask the family. Elderly relatives (there is usually at least one repository of family lore - often a spinster aunt) can save you aeons of time, or, of course, mislead you badly. Mine led me up a Welsh garden path, saying that her recipe for onion pudding was an old Welsh recipe she had from her mother. If you have a family bible with baptisms etc entered in it you are laughing - but just make sure that you confirm all the entries from official sources.

Genealogical Research Directory (Keith A Johnson and Malcolm Sainty) has been published annually since 1981. It lists the names and addresses of people worldwide currently working on families. Some are on the shelves in the PRO's library in the

Family Records Centre (FRC). You can consult the directories in good reference libraries and in Family History Centres of the Church of Jesus Christ of Latter-day Saints (LDS). The FRC holds a consolidated CD-ROM of all entries between 1990 and 1996.

Ancestral File (on the CD-ROM *FamilySearch*) can be consulted in the Family Records Centre and in LDS Family History Centres. It contains unauthenticated pedigrees submitted by members of the LDS Church.

The Society of Genealogists houses thousands of family trees, printed and manuscript, and family histories. Consult the catalogue in their library (see below p 5).

There is a microfiche index called BIG R (British Isles Genealogical Register). This is a consolidated index of names being researched, together with the names and addresses of contributors. The whole index or individual county sections can be purchased from the Federation of Family History Societies (see below); county sections are held by appropriate family history societies (see below). A copy of the second (1997) edition is in the FRC. Almost 220,000 entries make this an immensely useful aid.

Organisations which you should know about

Your local family history society

Ask about this in your local library or record office.

The Federation of Family History Societies at the Benson Room, Birmingham and Midland Institute, Margaret Street, Birmingham B3 3BS, co-ordinates a large number of family history societies which now exist. These societies meet regularly for support, exchange of information, outings and a lot of fun. Most publish journals. Write to the Federation with a SAE for more information. The Federation's half-yearly journal, *Family History News and Digest*, lists all the local societies. You can buy a copy in the shop at the Family Records Centre.

The Federation publishes a range of inexpensive guide books; you will find reference to them throughout this book. They can be bought in the bookshop at the Family Records Centre or ordered direct from FFHS Publications Limited, 2-4 Killer Street, Ramsbottom, Bury, Lancs BL0 9BZ.

Your local Church of Jesus Christ of Latter-day Saints (LDS) Family History Centre

The LDS Church has filmed and indexed vast runs of records vital to the pursuit of family history worldwide. At LDS Family History Centres throughout the country you can consult these films. Most have to be ordered from the LDS headquarters in Salt Lake City, Utah and take about a month to come. A small monthly fee is charged. All centres have a copy of the index to parish registers and other sources (the International Genealogical Index or IGI, described on p 48) and many have the CD-ROM program, *FamilySearch* (described on p 50).

For those who cannot spend time and money travelling to London and around the country, these centres offer an excellent local service.

Write with a SAE to the address below and ask for the name and address of your local centre: The Genealogical Society of Utah, British Isles Family History Service Centre, 185 Penns Lane, Sutton Coldfield, West Midlands B76 8JU.

The Society of Genealogists

The Society is very near to the Family Records Centre (see map) at 14 Charterhouse Buildings, Goswell Road, London EC1M 7BA (tel: 0171 251 8799). It has a library of published and unpublished source material of great value to the family historian. One of their most useful collections is the transcripts of many parish registers, listed by county in *Parish Register Copies in the Library of the Society of Genealogists*, 11th ed. 1995, which you can buy at the bookshop at the Centre.

You can join the society, paying an annual fee, or pay on a daily, hourly, or 4-hourly basis to use the library. The Centre sells *Using the Library of the Society of Genealogists*, 1997.

The Society also publishes a range of cheap, useful booklets which can be bought in the Family Records Centre shop or ordered direct from the Society.

Before you begin

How do I start doing my own research?

Let us suppose you have checked out what research has already been done, found nothing and so you are starting from scratch. ***The Family Records Centre is the place to come.***

In the General Register Office (GRO) search area (downstairs) you can order your own birth certificate - or that of your mother, father, grandparent of which ever line you fancy tracing. You can do that at the Family Records Centre (or local register office or by post, see pp 21-22) and then proceed from there, tracing your family back through birth, marriage and death certificates, supplementing these with census returns, wills and other records. This book will show you round the Family Records Centre and tell you how it is done.

The case studies on pp 96-110 will show you how to use certificates, census returns and other sources to research your family tree.

How far back will I get?

How long is a piece of string? If your family did not stray from England, Wales or Scotland you have a fair chance of getting back to the eighteenth century, perhaps to Tudor times. Before that the records are very uneven and the only serious chance you have of taking any line back into the Middle Ages is by linking it with some established pedigree, such as one of the official genealogies prepared by heralds in the early modern period.

Which line should I trace?

Any one you fancy. If you get stuck finding your father's father, try the maternal line instead. Most family historians these days branch out into as many lines as they can - four grandparents, eight great-grandparents and so on down the branches of the tree until you have hundreds of them!

What's in a name?

Obviously, common names present more difficulties than unusual ones. Trying to identify the 'right' John Smith can be a nightmare.

Surnames can be found in concentrations in specific parts of the country, *see* H B Guppy, *Homes of Family Names* (London, 1890 reprinted 1968) and the International Genealogical Index (explained on p 48).

There are a number of One Name Study Groups. Find out if there is one for your surname by writing to the Secretary, Guild of One Name Studies (GOONS), at Box G, Society of Genealogists, 14 Charterhouse Buildings, Goswell Road, London EC1M 7BA.

Before general literacy names were spoken rather than written down and there was no standard spelling. Even within the last hundred years Cockses and Coxes may be the same family. Shakespeare's name appears in seven different forms. Foreign names are more likely to be misheard or mangled by clergyman, immigration officer, census enumerator or whoever first wrote them down. Aliases were common until the eighteenth century; the use of an alias at a later date may indicate illegitimacy or adoption.

Welsh genealogy can be difficult because of the use of patronymics and the vast numbers of people with the same surname.

Far fewer *forenames* were regularly used than is the case today. John, Edward, Henry, Thomas, William, Mary, Elizabeth and Ann were the most common. The tradition of naming eldest sons after their father and eldest daughters after their mother and subsequent children after their grandparents can prove useful in forging links. Sons, especially second sons, might be given their mother's maiden name as their first or second forename.

It is important to remember that in the days of widespread infant mortality it was very common for parents to give a child the name of a deceased brother or sister.

Some facts about Victorian families which will help you in your research

As much of your genealogical research here is probably going to be into your nineteenth century forebears, it is worth bearing a few things in mind.

- Families could be very large - your great-great-grandmother may have been producing babies regularly over twenty years or more.

- Infant mortality was very high.

- Working class couples did not always marry. If they did it was commonly after the birth of the first child.

- Don't assume your great-greats were only married once. Life was shorter and more precarious than it subsequently became and second and third marriages were quite as common as they are now.

- Weddings in the register office (started 1 July 1837) for some carried the stigma of the Poor Law. Marriages between couples of different denominations were more likely to be in register offices than the Established Church.

- Don't assume that your family stayed put in one place. People moved around looking for work, especially after industrialisation and the coming of the railways.

THE FAMILY RECORDS CENTRE (FRC)

The Centre is the new 'St Catherine's House'; it combines the public search room of the Office for National Statistics' General Register Office, which holds birth, marriage and death indexes for England and Wales from 1 July 1837 and indexes of registrations of 'vital events' of British citizens abroad going back to the eighteenth century, and the census and wills rooms of the Public Record Office, which used to be in Chancery Lane.

The ONS search room is on the ground floor and there you can consult the indexes and order certificates (£6.50 each; they will be ready to collect in four working days) which will give you the information you need (see p 21 ff). At the back of the room is the Scottish Link area, where you can book one of the computers, pay for up to two hours' consecutive research of prime genealogical sources for Scottish ancestors and order copies of records from Edinburgh.

The PRO search room is on the first floor. There you can read various sources on film to complement and extend what you have found downstairs. There is immediate access to the PRO material - you find what you want in the indexes and help yourself to film or fiche.

Genealogical compilations of material on the LDS program known as *FamilySearch*, available on CD-ROM, including the latest editions of the International Genealogical Index (the IGI), and other personal name indexes can be inspected at the Centre.

There is a shop in the entrance lobby where you can buy a wide range of family history guides. You can use the small well-stocked library, the advisory service, and on-the-spot copying facilities; there are refreshment areas with vending machines, meeting room, lockers to stow away your belongings (if you want to), baby changing room and public telephones. Parking is available nearby on meters and in public car parks and there is an abundance of public transport. On site there is limited disabled car parking, which must be reserved in advance (tel: 0171 533 6436).

The Centre is a few minutes' walk from London Metropolitan Archives (formerly the Greater London Record Office) and the Society of Genealogists.

SOURCES IN THE FAMILY RECORDS CENTRE

General Register Office, Office for National Statistics (ground floor):

The ONS holds **indexes** to the following records:

Births, marriages and deaths registered in England and Wales from 1 July 1837

Adoptions registered in England and Wales since 1927

Births and deaths at sea (Marine) registered from July 1837 until 1965

Regimental (1761-1924), army chaplains returns and Service Department registers of births, deaths and marriages (1796-1965)

RAF returns of births, marriages and deaths from 1920 (with Army Returns to 1950 for deaths, to 1955 for births, to 1949 for marriages, and then in Service Department indexes up to 1965)

Royal Naval returns of births, marriages and deaths from 1959

Consular returns of births, marriages and deaths for British citizens abroad from July 1849 until 1965

Civil aviation births and deaths and missing (presumed dead) from 1947 until 1965

High Commission returns of births and deaths from the date of the independence of the Commonwealth country up to 1965

Military and civil registers, Chaplains' Register Ionian Islands, births, marriages and deaths, 1818-64

Online access to birth and death indexes 1984-1992 and marriages 1984-1993

From 1966 all births, marriages and deaths abroad are indexed in union volumes for each event.

War deaths:

> *Natal and South Africa Forces, Boer War (1899 -1902)*
> *First World War (1914-1921) - Army officers, other ranks*
> *(including RAF); Naval, all ranks (including RAF);*
> *Indian services war deaths (1914-21)*
> *Second World War (3 September 1939 - 30 June 1948) -*
> *Army officers, other ranks; Naval officers, ratings;*
> *Royal Air Force, all ranks; Indian Services war deaths*
> *(1939-1948)*

(These records include deaths after the wars which have resulted from injuries received in conflicts.)

Only the indexes to the registrations are available at the FRC. Information from the registrations is available in the form of a certificate, for which a fee must be paid.

The Scottish Link (ground floor)

This has **indexes** to the following records:

> *Births, marriages and deaths 1855 to date; integrated with indexes to adoption registers from 1930*
>
> *Divorce files 1984 to date*
>
> *Old parish registers 1553-1854*
>
> *1891 census returns*
>
> *1881 census returns*

These indexes are on line and can be searched for a fee. Certificates and copies from the original records may then be ordered direct from Edinburgh (see below p 39).

The Public Record Office (first floor)

Microfilm copies of census returns, 1841, 1851, 1861, 1871, 1881 (with microfiche name index), 1891 (also on microfiche)

Microfilms of Death Duty registers 1796-1857, indexes 1796-1903

Microfilms of wills and administrations, 1383-1858 (Prerogative Court of Canterbury (PCC) only)

Microfiche of the calendar of wills proved from January 1858-1943

Microfilms of many Nonconformist registers 1567-1837

Microfilm indexes of miscellaneous foreign returns of births, deaths and marriages from 1627-1960

Microfiche of the British Isles Genealogical Register of families and places currently being researched, 1997

Microfiche copies of the LDS International Genealogical Index (IGI), Great Britain only, 1992 edition

FamilySearch CD-ROM; worldwide genealogical data: Ancestral File, 1993 edition of the IGI, with addenda

Genealogical Research Directory 1990-1996 on CD-ROM, encompassing families being researched worldwide

Access to the records is free. Photocopies may be purchased if required of material on microfiche and microfilm.

IMPORTANT SOURCES *NOT* IN THE FAMILY RECORDS CENTRE

Parish registers (England, Wales and Scotland) for pre-1837 births, marriages and deaths

The evidence from parish registers provides the main building blocks of family history for the period before central registration of births, marriages and deaths was introduced (1837). They are not available in the FRC, but the IGI contains millions of entries with which you can make a start.

Since the sixteenth century Church of England parishes have kept registers of baptisms, marriages and burials. From the seventeenth century, in addition, Nonconformist chapels started to register births, baptisms and burials of members. Until the mid-19th century the vast majority of people came under the auspices of the Church of England. In Scotland parochial registers began slightly later, and births as well as baptisms were recorded. Burial entries tend to be less thoroughly written up.

Millions of baptismal and marriage entries have been indexed by the Church of Jesus Christ of Latter-day Saints (LDS); these indexes (the International Genealogical Index or IGI) are available in fiche and CD-ROM form in the PRO's research area at the FRC (*see* pp 48-51). The Scottish births, baptisms and marriages in the Church of Scotland parochial registers up to 1854 may be accessed via CD-ROM on *FamilySearch*, and the computerised index on Scottish link.

Check these indexes first.

Most parish (Church of England) registers are now in local record offices. To locate the ones you want you could consult *The Phillimore Atlas and Index of Parish Registers* edited by C R Humphery-Smith (Chichester 2nd ed. 1995) on the shelves in the library of the PRO, on the first floor of the FRC. This book will also tell you if there is a transcript in the library of the Society of Genealogists (near to the FRC, *see* p 5 and the map on p vi). J Gibson and P Peskett's *Record Offices: How to Find Them* (Federation of Family History Societies, 8th ed. 1998; also in the library) will give you the address and phone number of the appropriate record office. Always check by telephoning the record office concerned; you may have to book a seat. *The Atlas* records which English, Welsh and Scottish parishes are in the 1992 IGI.

Authenticated Nonconformist chapel registers of England and Wales are in the PRO/ FRC; other chapel registers are at PRO Kew or held locally (*see* pp 89 ff). Those on microfilm at the Centre are integrated into the 1992 IGI, as indicated in *The Atlas* above.

A number of Welsh registers are held in the National Library of Wales at Aberystwyth. Look at *The Atlas* for details of dates and whereabouts.

A complete list of Scottish Old Parochial Registers can be found in *The Atlas*, too.

A note on marriage entries

Marriages tend to be difficult to find; they frequently take place in the bride's parish church and the couple then move to the groom's place of residence or somewhere else entirely.

The IGI (*see* p 48) contains marriages as well as baptisms. Your first attempt when looking for a pre-1837 marriage might well be the CD-ROM *FamilySearch*.

Many family history societies have compiled county marriage indexes. There is also a number of marriage indexes in private hands which can be searched for you for a small fee. Known marriage indexes are listed in J Gibson and E Hampson *Marriage and Census Indexes for Family Historians* (Federation of Family History Societies, 7th ed. 1998). This covers the entire British Isles.

A number of marriages were conducted by licence rather than banns. Known indexes to marriage licence allegations and bonds, and a list of the whereabouts of the documents themselves can be traced in J Gibson, *Bishops' Transcripts and Marriage Licences: A Guide to their Location and Indexes* (FFHS, 4th ed. 1997).

Boyds's marriage index, which covers millions of pre-1837 marriages in England, can be consulted in the census library on the first floor of the Centre. There are separate indexes for grooms and brides, so each marriage is recorded twice. The index to brides goes up to 1850, for grooms up to 1837 (N... is the last surname after 1800). Look at *A List of Parishes in Boyd's Marriage Index* (SOG, 1992, reprinted with minor corrections, 1994), a copy of which is nearby.

Records of Irish Ancestors

Many of the records you need for Irish family history are in Ireland. Buy one of the guides to Irish genealogy in the bookshop. Try the IGI as well.

For birth, marriage and death records for the whole of Ireland from 1864 (non-Roman Catholic marriages from 1845) until 1921, and for Eire to date, apply to the General Register Office of Ireland, Joyce House, 8-11 Lombard Street, Dublin 2, Ireland, tel: 003531 6711863. Indexes are held at LDS Family History Centres (*see* p 5) too.

Records of birth, marriage and death in Northern Ireland from 1 January 1922 are with the Registrar General in Belfast at the General Register Office (Northern Ireland), Oxford House, Chichester Street, Belfast BT1 4HL, tel: 01232 235211.

Census returns and other records are held in the National Archives of Ireland, Bishop Street, Dublin 8, tel: 003531 478 3711. The 1901 and 1911 censuses have been filmed and the films may be ordered from Salt Lake City and read at LDS Family History Centres (*see* p 5). Only fragments of earlier decadal returns from 1841 now survive.

The service records of men who served in the Royal Irish Constabulary are at PRO Kew (*see* p 16), as are those of Irishmen who served in the British Army and Royal Navy.

The Society of Genealogists has some useful material. *See* Anthony Camp's *Sources for Irish Genealogy in the Library of the Society of Genealogists* (SOG, 2nd ed. 1997)

Records of ancestors in India

Ecclesiastical returns of births/baptisms, marriages, deaths and burials of British people in India from the late seventeenth century to 1947, and a few between 1948 and 1952, are kept in the India Office Library along with registered wills, and a variety of other sources about East India Company employees and British residents, indexes and reference works. The library (properly called the British Library Oriental and India Office Collections), presently at 197 Blackfriars Road, London SE1 8NG, tel: 0171 412 7873 moves to The British Library, 96 Euston Road, St Pancras, London NW1 2DB in August 1998.

Wills from 1858 (England and Wales)

Wills proved from January 1858 can be read at the Principal Probate Registry of the Family Division which is, at present, in the Strand, London WC2R 9LP, near Waterloo Bridge, tel: 0171-936-7000. It is due to be relocated in June 1998 to First Avenue House, 42-49 High Holborn, London WC1V 6HA. You are advised to check before visiting. For more about wills see pp 65 ff.

Divorce records

From 1858 to 1940 these are at PRO Kew (indexes to 1958). From about 1941 a search will be done for you, for a fee, at the Divorce Registry at Somerset House, London WC2R 1LP. See *New to Kew?* pp 63-4.

Probate records (Prerogative Court of Canterbury, PCC)

Although wills and grants of administration from the PCC up to 11 January 1858 may be read at both the FRC and PRO Kew, supporting probate material such as inventories and the records of contested probates in this court may be read only at PRO Kew (*see* pp 65ff). They are described in Miriam Scott's *Prerogative Court of Canterbury: Wills and Other Probate Records* (PRO Publications, 1997).

Records of men serving in the armed forces from the eighteenth century

Personnel records about millions of British soldiers and sailors provide an invaluable genealogical source. Each service kept details about officers and men and their families and these may help to extend the family tree for you or to liven up the family story!

The records are kept at PRO Kew and are described in the companion to this volume, *New to Kew?* Also useful is *Army Service Records of the First World War* by Simon Fowler, William Spencer and Stuart Tamblin (PRO Publications, 1997).

Death Duty records (England and Wales) 1858-1903

If you have found a will or grant of administration for your ancestor in the Principal Probate Registry, it is well worth looking at the corresponding Death Duty entry - it may add quite a lot about his estate and members of the family. Death Duty records in general are described on pp 79 ff).

The records from 1858 may be read at PRO Kew, but you need to give five days' notice when requesting them, as they are stored off-site. Look at J Cox, *An Introduction to ... Affection Defying the Power of Death: Wills, Probate and Death Duty Records* (FFHS, 1993, reprinted 1995).

Other important sources at PRO Kew

Many more sources are available at PRO Kew. Those most used by family historians are described in the companion volume to this book, *New to Kew?* These are:

Apprenticeship records 18th century

Births, marriages and deaths of Britons abroad, 1627 to 1965, some (see also p 94)

Cemetery records

Change of name records from 1760

Coastguard service records 19th and 20th century

Crime: convicts and transportation registers 18th and 19th century

Customs and Excise Officers' service records 17th to 20th century

Dockyard workers' records 17th to 19th century

Emigrants' records 17th to 20th century

Immigrants' records 17th to 20th century

Legal records: civil actions from medieval times

Maps and tithe records

Marriage - 'Fleet' and other irregular marriages in London 1667 - 24 March 1754

Medieval records

Merchant seamen's records

Nonconformist records, 17th to 20th century, some

Nurses' records 20th century

Police (London Metropolitan and Royal Irish Constabulary) service records 19th and 20th century

Railway workers' service records 19th and 20th century

Tax lists medieval to 20th century

Two full guides to the PRO's genealogical holdings are *Tracing your Ancestors in the Public Record Office* (4th ed, HMSO, 1990, a new edition of which will be published in late 1998), and S Colwell, *A Dictionary of Genealogical Sources in the Public Record Office* (Weidenfeld and Nicolson, 1992). A comprehensive guide to the PRO's holdings is *The Public Record Office Guide*, which has been published on microfiche (PRO Publications, 1996) and should be available in most good reference libraries. The third part of this is a subject index leading you to administrative histories of the records in part one, which explain the background to the creation and evolution of the departmental archives, and descriptions of record classes in part two which give brief summaries of the period and content of each group of documents.

USING THE CENTRE

Access

As you will see from the map on p vi the Centre is readily accessible and near to central London. It is open to all - there are no readers' tickets. It is open six days a week, with two late evenings, on Tuesday and Thursday.

Facilities

There are numerous cafes and restaurants nearby, and drinks machines and a refreshment area in the building.

The bookshop offers a wide range of family history guides.

The Centre has plentiful photocopying facilities, public telephones, access for the disabled and a baby changing room.

What should I take to the Centre?

Take any notes you have already made, pen and paper. Make sure that you put your name and address on your research papers in case you misplace them. If you don't want to waste precious time going outside to a restaurant or cafe, take some sandwiches - you can eat them in the basement refreshment area.

Wear comfortable shoes. If you are going to be searching the indexes in the GRO search area, you will be on your feet a good deal.

Try to avoid busy periods such as lunchtimes, as you will be competing with your fellow family historians.

A gazetteer or atlas is a good idea. You are going to find your ancestors in places you have never heard of and you will need to check out where they are, to make sure you have got the right people! The Centre does, however, have copies on the premises.

You will need cash/credit cards/cheque book with cheque card for photocopies and to buy certificates.

The surrounding area

Although the Centre is housed in a brand new building, it is in a part of London redolent of the past; Clerkenwell is one of the oldest and most rumbustious of the City's suburbs, a red-light district in Shakespeare's day and traditionally associated with Huguenot watch makers and Italian immigrants. It is a vibrant area with a market and plenty of cafes, restaurants and good, old-fashioned pubs.

The Society of Genealogists is nearby (see above p 5 and map on p vi). You can join or buy a day's research in the splendid library with its unrivalled collection of parish register transcripts and other things to browse amongst.

If your ancestors were Londoners (most families have some people in London at some stage) you could stroll over to the London Metropolitan Archives (40 Northampton Road, London EC1R OHB; tel: 0171 332 3822. See map on p vi) where you will find many of the London parish registers, the Middlesex deeds registry, some Londoners' wills, a terrific map and photograph collection, a good library, advice on London ancestry and much else besides.

PART II
The Office for National Statistics
Search Area

Family Records Centre - Ground Floor

Plan of the ONS search area

1   Customer service desk
     Certificate collection
     Tills, Manager
2   Public seating area
3   Births
4   Marriages
5   Deaths
6   Adoptions
     Overseas registrations

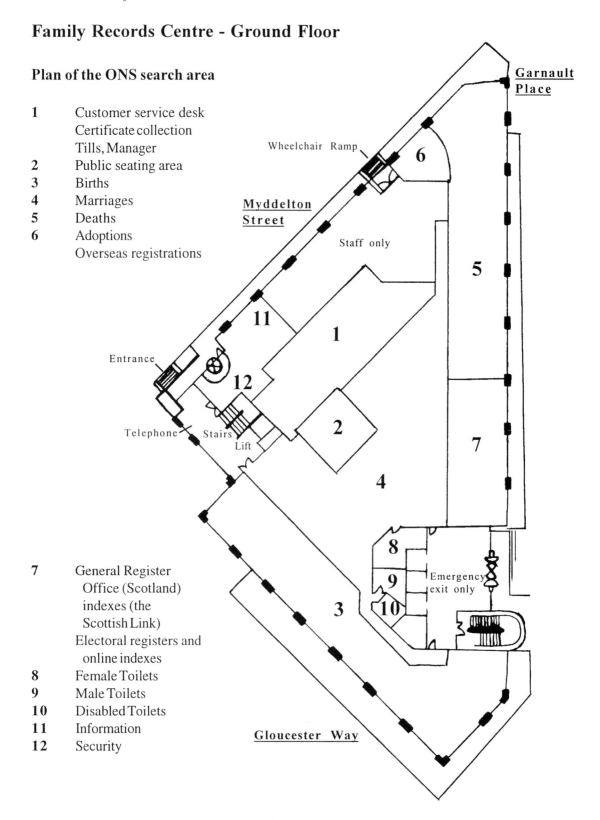

7   General Register
     Office (Scotland)
     indexes (the
     Scottish Link)
     Electoral registers and
     online indexes
8   Female Toilets
9   Male Toilets
10   Disabled Toilets
11   Information
12   Security

Indexes of births, marriages and deaths

England and Wales

The General Register Office (GRO) holds indexes to:

> **registers of births, marriages and deaths in England and Wales from 1 July 1837**

> **registers of adoption from 1927**

*Only the **indexes** to the GRO records are available at the FRC. No indexes are available for pre-1796 Army marriages (see p 33). The GRO also holds registrations of stillbirths which have occurred since 1927. However these are not available to the general public, and indexes are not on show in the FRC. Details about stillbirths will be revealed only with the consent of the Registrar General to the parents or*

siblings when both parents are dead. The records are kept by the ONS, Certificate Services, at Southport, telephone 0151 471 4800.

To get the full genealogical data you will need to buy a certificate which gives you the information from the original registration. Certificates will be available for collection at the FRC in four working days. Alternatively they can be posted to you by first class post after three working days. Some family history societies and individuals offer a courier service.

There is a priority service for those who need certificates urgently. They are available one working day after application and there is an additional fee payable.

Searching in the indexes for births, marriages and deaths in England and Wales from 1837

Births, marriages and deaths were centrally registered from 1 July 1837.

The indexes give you the name of the individual concerned, the quarter of the year when the event was registered (until 1984 when annual indexes were first produced), the registration district, the volume number of the original register and the number of the page in that volume where the entry is. (*See* Parr entries on p 24).

Using indexes near home

If you live out of London there is no need to come to the FRC to consult these indexes; they are widely available in local libraries and LDS Family History Centres. Be warned, however, that not all hold full sets.

Having found your entry in the indexes write to the address below with the exact reference and a cheque for £9 (£6.50 if you apply to the local register office, *see under* 'Registration of births, deaths and marriages' in your local telephone directory) and you will be sent a certificate. If you prefer to do the whole thing by post (not advisable if you have a lot of research to carry out), you can apply to the address, giving what details you have and ask for a search to be made for you. The current charge for a five-year search, to include a certificate, is £12.

Certificate charges are regularly reviewed.

> General Register Office
> PO Box 2
> Southport
> Merseyside
> PR8 2JD

GRO's enquiry line is 0151 471 4800.

Searching the ONS indexes

The indexes are in large volumes. A microfiche set is available for researchers who find using the indexes difficult. Telephone 0171 533 6438 to book a time slot.

There is a system of colour coding for the volumes, which you will find on shelves in the search area:

> Red indexes for births
> Green indexes for marriages
> Black indexes for deaths

The indexes are arranged alphabetically in quarterly volumes (until after 1983), and labelled accordingly:

> March (events registered in January, February, March).
> June (events registered in April, May, June).
> September (events registered in July, August, September).
> December (events registered in October, November, December).

Indexes from 1984 onwards are arranged alphabetically according to the year of registration.

Take the indexes, one by one from the shelves (if you are unable to handle these large volumes ask at the Scottish Link desk if you may use the fiche version). Go through them searching for your 'vital' event. All index entries give the **registration district** of the event, not the actual village or town where it happened (*see* below).

Marriages are registered at the time they happen but births and deaths (especially the former) may be registered some time later. Births should be registered within six weeks of the event.

Birth indexes are handwritten before 1865; from the September quarter of 1911 they give the maiden surname of the child's mother.

Marriage indexes do not give the names of both bride and groom together in each entry until 1912. Women are indexed by the name they were using at the time of marriage. For previously unmarried women this will be their maiden name. However, if a woman had been previously married and continued to use her previous married name at the time of her marriage (for example if she was a widow) she would be indexed under that.

Death indexes give the age of the deceased from 1865 and the date of birth from April 1969. Thus, supposing you know your grandfather died in 1950, look him up in the indexes and find out that he was 70. You can now look for his birth in the red indexes for 1880 (don't rely too much on the age given - just use it as a rough guide).

How do I know if I have got the right entry?

There will often be a number of people with the same name being born, married or dying in the same quarter.

	Registration District	Volume Number	Page Number
PARR Robert	Plymouth	5d	231
PARR Robert	Hackney	2d	342
PARR Robert	Rochdale	8b	435
PARR Robert	Colne	8b	534
PARR Robert	Birmingham	6c	654
PARR Robert	Birmingham	6c	987

You will need to know the **registration district** (RD) where your event happened. There are two maps on the walls showing registration districts 1837-1851 and 1852-1946; you can buy copies of these at the Scottish Link desk. RDs correspond roughly to the size of a medium-sized town. If you are looking for a village entry you may find that it is in a RD which bears the name of a nearby market town. If you have a query about registration districts you can ask at the customer service desk where there is a complete index of addresses and telephone numbers of current RDs, and a list of places giving the RDs to which they belong. In the PRO reading room on the first floor there is a copy of *An Index to Civil Registration Districts of England and Wales, 1837 to date*, compiled by J A Newport, 1989, which lists every district change since registration began. Ask at the enquiry desk upstairs.

If you find two or more events for your name in the same registration district in the same quarter - like the two Birmingham Robert Parrs above - then you can do a reference check. This is explained opposite.

Applying for a certificate

When you have found the birth, marriage or death, fill in one of the application forms in the nearby boxes (pink for birth, green for marriage, mauve for death), taking the details from the index (*see* Parr sample entry above).

If it is a birth certificate make sure you order a full certificate and not a short one (see below).

Take the form with your money (£6.50), cheque book (with card) or credit card to one of the windows in the tills area. You will be given a receipt which tells you when the certificate will be ready for you to collect - or it may be posted to you if you prefer. It will be ready in four working days.

Reference checking

If there are several entries which might be the right one, you can ask for a reference check, where the staff look at various entries in the original registers for you. First of all fill in an application form with the first reference you would like checked. You must fill in the back of the form with some extra information which the ONS staff can use to identify your entry. For example you might know the exact date of birth or the parents' forenames. You should then fill in a reference checking sheet, obtainable from the customer service desk, listing all of the other references you would like to have checked in order of likelihood. You will have to pay £6.50 for the first reference, as normal, and £3 for each of the other references you list.

On the bottom of the reference checking sheet you have two options: 1) Check all the references and 2) Stop at first that applies. If you choose the first option, all the references will be checked before a certificate is produced of the first corresponding entry (if this is possible). If you choose the second option, the references will be checked until an entry is found where the details agree with the information. In this case, you will receive a refund of £3 for each reference which was not checked. Only include such information about which you are certain, since the searches are specific.

Another form of reference check is where there is only one entry in the index, but you are still not sure if this is the one you want. In this case complete an application form as normal, but fill in the back of the form with any extra identifying information. The ONS staff will check the entry and only issue the certificate if the information ties up exactly with your details. If it does not, no certificate will be issued and you will get a £3 refund.

Don't be tempted to guess when putting information down, as you may not get a certificate which in fact might be the one you are looking for! Also be careful about using father's occupation as a checking point for marriage certificates. People's occupations can change over time, and the details in the entry may not be the same as the information you have got from another source.

As mentioned above, you might know from some other source the exact date of birth or the name of the parent. In the case of the two Robert Parrs born in Birmingham, let us suppose your Robert Parr's mother's first name was Martha. Put this on the back of the application form and the certificate will only be produced if one of those Robert Parrs in the index has a mother whose name in the entry is Martha.

Information on the certificates

Samples of different types of certificates are reproduced in the case studies (pp 96-110).

The information varies slightly according to the date of the certificate.

Birth and death certificates changed format in 1969. Birth certificates from that date on include the child's surname. Prior to 1969 no surname was given and it was assumed from the surname of the parents. In addition the post-1969 certificate will include details of the place of birth of both parents, and of both the mother's maiden name and the name she was using when she married for the last time if she had been married more than once. All full certificates, from 1837 onwards, will include the child's forename (if one had been given at the time of registration) and the exact date and place of birth. It will also disclose the mother's maiden name and may also set out the father's name and occupation. All certificates show the name and address of the informant of the registration; this is usually one of the parents. The mother's occupation, if she had one, may also be shown. Short birth certificates, with no details of parentage, were introduced as an option for those

wanting copies mainly for administrative purposes in 1947. They are no use for family history. Make sure you order a **full certificate**.

The informant for a death registration in 1837 was required to supply the date, place, name, age, sex, occupation and cause of death of the deceased. The death certificate of a married or widowed woman will also include the name and occupation of her husband. Before 1874 the cause of death might be a guess; thereafter a medical certificate was required so it is more likely to be reliable. Certificates of deaths which have taken place since 1 April 1969 also include the date and place of birth, usual address and the maiden name of a married woman.

Marriage certificates have not changed since 1837. They include the names, marital status and occupation (if any) of both parties, as well as their ages. Unfortunately, this was sometimes recorded as 'over 21' or 'of full age'. The certificates will also include the addresses of both parties, and the names and occupations of their fathers.

Be wary of accepting all the information at its face value. Remember people lie about their age, for a variety of reasons and, in the past, would not necessarily be sure how old they were. The ages of women on marriage certificates should be treated with caution and ages given on death certificates may often be very rough estimates - would the family necessarily have any idea how old grandpa was? Addresses on marriage certificates are notoriously unreliable - they still are. How often do couples 'establish residence' somewhere where they don't live at all to get married in a certain church? The stated occupations of grooms and the fathers of both brides and grooms may be exaggerations or downright lies especially if one of the parties concerned was anxious to impress new in-laws.

'Missing' births, marriages and deaths

Most experienced family historians have at least one ancestor whose birth, death or marriage they have diligently sought for years without success. Some of the common explanations why you can't find an event which must be there are given below.

You are looking under Coom and the event is entered under Combe. Check alternative **spellings of names**.

The event happened in a **different year** from the one you have searched. Perhaps you are looking for the birth of Ann Layzell in 1842/3 because she told the census enumerator that she was 39 (in 1881) when she was really 43! Census ages can be wildly out.

Some births were just **never registered** - especially among the poor, labouring folk in big cities. There are a particularly large number of omissions pre-1875 (as many as 15% of births may have gone unregistered) when there was no penalty for non-registration. You could try looking in the baptismal registers of the local church or chapel (see pp 89 ff) - in the days of the great Victorian religious revival and high infant mortality mothers were anxious to secure a place in heaven for their babies. Registration-dodging went on until 1940 when evidence of registration was needed for the issue of ration books.

You may be looking for a birth under the **wrong forename**. Perhaps you are looking for someone known to the family as Albert Jennings. Actually his full name was Maurice Albert and he appears in the indexes under Jennings, Maurice A. Perhaps you are looking for Peggy Drew under Drew, P, when her name was, of course, really Margaret.

Babies registered **without a forename** (perhaps the parents could not agree or the baby died soon after birth) appear at the end of the alphabetical list of surnames simply as 'male' or 'female'. Thus you might be looking for a George Staines under Staines, G. He didn't get the name George until he was six months old, perhaps, so he will appear at the end of the Staineses in the index.

Babies born outside marriage might be registered under the **mother's maiden name**.

Perhaps your ancestor was born under a completely different name from that by which he subsequently became known; he may have been **adopted**. See under 'Adoption' below.

You can't find a marriage for a couple you know had children. Perhaps you started searching backwards from the date of the birth of the eldest child (that is what researchers tend to do). Perhaps you should go the other way; it has been estimated that in the nineteenth century about **10% of marriages took place after the birth of the first child**.

Possibly they **never married** at all. This is more common than you might imagine. Henry Mayhew, writing in the mid-nineteenth century, said that among the 'costers' of London, marriage was the norm only for Roman Catholics and Jews.

You are looking for a marriage under the known maiden name of an ancestress. Maybe she had been **married before** she married your great-grandfather, and used her former wedded name.

The event you are looking for happened **abroad, or in Scotland or Ireland**. If abroad you can search the foreign indexes (see p 30), if in Scotland you can try the FRC's Scottish Link (see p 38), if in Ireland there's not much you can do about it here (see p 13) but details of births registered between 1864 and 1875 are included on the IGI.

Births outside marriage

Births outside marriage are usually registered by the mother with a blank where the father's name should be. If the parents were living as man and wife then the father's name will probably appear. Before 1874 the mother could name anyone she liked as the father of her child and the registrar was bound to accept it. After that the name of the father was only put in the register if he went with the mother to register the birth; in this case both of them will have signed the register entry. Alternatively, a statutory declaration acknowledging paternity could be produced. In both cases the father's name was only inserted with his consent.

If there is no hint in family lore as to who the father might be, you are in trouble and are probably best advised to pursue the female line. You may find reference to the father in Poor Law Union records which are deposited in local record offices. The Poor Law Union Boards of Guardians were the 'Child Support Agency' of the past, whose job it was to prevent children being supported from the rates if the father could be identified and tracked down.

If there is a family tradition which suggests that the child was sired by the local 'lord of the manor' or some famous person, then it may be worth checking the will of the supposed father and also the Death Duty Registers (*see* p 79 ff). The latter have a 'consanguinity column' which explains the exact nature of the relationship between the beneficiary and the deceased.

See also under 'Adoption' p 35.

Births, marriages and deaths of British citizens abroad

These events are scattered in different libraries and record offices. Be prepared to dig around.

The main series of records relating to British nationals in foreign countries are held by the ONS with indexes in the FRC.

Others are at PRO Kew, in the Guildhall Library, the Society of Genealogists and other places. If you have failed to find your event in the ONS indexes you should go upstairs to the PRO's census library and look through the lists in the three following books, *Tracing your Ancestors in the Public Record Office* (HMSO 4th ed. 1990, 4th impression 1995, pp 48-62), *Dictionary of Genealogical Sources in the Public Record Office* and *The British Overseas, Guildhall Library Research Guide 2* (3rd, revised ed. 1994).

Events in ex-colonies

In the PRO area there is a microfilm index of miscellaneous births, marriages and deaths of Britons abroad, registers of which are at the PRO, Kew from 1627 to 1967. The registers are released to Kew when they are 30 years old, so 1968 will be added in January 1999.

If your family lived in a country which was formerly a British colony, then the chances are that the 'vital events' which happened to them when they were there are recorded in the registry of that country. You will have to write off to the country concerned. Consult T J Kemp, *International Vital Records Handbook*, 3rd ed. 1995, in the PRO's library on the first floor, or ask at the ONS customer service desk for an up-to-date list of addresses to write to.

*Events in **India** (to 1948) should be sought in the India Office and Oriental Collections of the British Library (see p 94).*

The Overseas Section of the ONS

The overseas section in the ONS public search room is marked on the plan. There you will find an assorted series of indexes of births (red bound), marriages (green bound) and deaths (black bound). From 1966 there is a single series for all births, all marriages and all deaths. Before that date check you are looking in the right subject volumes.

The ONS holds:

> *Births and deaths at sea (Marine) registered from July 1837 until 1965*
>
> *Regimental (1761-1924), army chaplains returns and Service Department registers of births, deaths and marriages (1796-1965)*
>
> *RAF returns of births, marriages and deaths from 1920 (with Army Returns to 1950 for deaths, to 1955 for births, to 1949 for marriages, and then in Service Department indexes up to 1965)*
>
> *Royal Naval returns of births, marriages and deaths from 1959*
>
> *Consular returns of births, marriages and deaths for British citizens abroad from July 1849 until 1965*
>
> *Civil aviation births and deaths and missing (presumed dead) from 1947 until 1965.*
>
> *High Commission returns of births and deaths from the date of the independence of the Commonwealth country up to 1965*
>
> *Military and civil registers, Chaplains' Register Ionian Islands, births, marriages and deaths, 1818-64*
>
> *From 1966 all births, marriages and deaths abroad are indexed in union volumes for each event*
>
> *War deaths:*
> > *Natal and South Africa Forces, Boer War (1899 -1902)*
> > *First World War (1914-1921) - Army officers, other ranks (including RAF); Naval, all ranks (including RAF); Indian services war deaths (1914-21)*

**Second World War (3 September 1939 - 30 June 1948) -
Army officers, other ranks; Naval officers, ratings;
Royal Air Force, all ranks; Indian Services war deaths
(1939-1948)**

(These records include deaths after the wars which have resulted from injuries received in conflicts.)

If you find your 'event' you fill in an 'overseas' application form and pay £6.50 at one of the tills. A certificate, containing information from the original registers, will be prepared for you. You can ask for it to be posted to you or collect it next time you come in. It may take a little longer than the four days it takes for an ordinary certificate.

If you have any problems phone the Overseas Section at the GRO, tel: 0151 471 4801.

Records of births and deaths at sea from July 1837

The return of the event might be in different forms. The ONS will include only the usual details found on a 'home' certificate.

There is another, more complete, series of marine registers at PRO Kew (refs. BT 158, BT 159, BT 160 (births 1875-1891). It is best to start with the ONS indexes.

Registers of marriages on naval ships for the period 1842-1889 can be read on film in the PRO at Kew (ref RG 33/156, index in RG 43/7 at the Centre).

There is a time-honoured tradition which says births and deaths on merchant vessels were entered in the parish registers of the church of St Dunstan, Stepney. They were not, and I can only think the story grew up because the parish used to be crammed full of sailors; St Dunstan's is still known as the 'Church of the High Seas'.

Army returns from 1761

These records relate to the marriages of men serving in the British Army and Navy (from 1881), children born to them and deaths of men and their families which occurred abroad and some of those at home. Other deaths at home will be found among the ordinary indexes (from 1837). War deaths are kept separately (*see* below).

The army returns are actually in four series to 1965 (Regimental Returns, Army Chaplains Returns, Army Returns, and Service Departments). The 'Regimental Returns' of marriages cover the period 1761 to 1924; some of them are set out as 'family returns' which include details of the children of the marriage. The marriages themselves have no available index though you can search indexes of births/baptisms and deaths. If you want the record of an army marriage from this period you will need to know the regiment your ancestor was in. Write to the Overseas Section of the ONS at Southport (address on p 22) with this information and they will make a search for you in the records of that regiment and if successful, will supply a certificate for £6.50. The ONS is unable to reproduce the entire family return but can identify children. A list of regiments and their records is available in the Overseas Area at the Centre.

For all other events, proceed as you would when ordering an ordinary birth, marriage or death certificate, but using the special application forms supplied for overseas.

RAF returns from 1920

The RAF came into being on 1 April 1918. Before this date the flying force consisted of the Royal Flying Corps, under the auspices of the Army, and the Royal Naval Air Service, a branch of the Royal Navy.

The returns are of the marriages and deaths of RAF personnel and the birth of their children. These are indexed with Army Returns up to 1949 for marriages, 1950 for deaths, and 1955 for births, then up to 1965 in the indexes to the Service Departments' registers. Thereafter they can be found in union indexes of all births, marriages and deaths of Britons abroad. War deaths are in separate series (*see* below).

Find your 'event' and order a certificate in the usual way.

Royal Naval returns from 1959

Naval returns of births, deaths and marriages from 1959 are included in the Service Department indexes; after 1965 they are accessed via union indexes of all births, marriages and deaths of Britons abroad.

Consular Returns from 1849

These are births, marriages and deaths of Britons in foreign countries, registered by the British consul. In all instances the places given in the indexes to records are to the place where the event was registered, not where it happened.

If you cannot find your event in the indexes, there are various other places to explore. The PRO, on the first floor, has miscellaneous indexes to registers held at the PRO, Kew which you can read on film; these are listed in detail in *Tracing your Ancestors in the Public Record Office* and *Dictionary of Genealogical Sources in the Public Record Office* (cited above) which you can consult in the PRO's library. Other extant returns are listed in *The British Overseas* (cited above).

Registration was voluntary, so your event may not necessarily be among these records; there may be a record of it in the country concerned. Ask to see the list of addresses of foreign registrars general, or consult *International Vital Records Handbook* (cited above), in the PRO's census library.

Civil aviation births and deaths, 1947-65

These were registers compiled under the Civil Aviation Act 1949, and set out the name, place, year and page reference to each entry. Ages are included for deceased individuals. There is a separate index at the end of the book for Missing Persons, which records name, age, place or aircraft missing, the year and page reference.

High Commission returns

United Kingdom High Commission (UKHC) indexes to births to 1966 appear to start about 1934, and these record name, place, year, type of post, volume and page, so you can find out about British subjects whose births were registered with the High Commissioners. Some of the entries for 1966 are duplicated in the indexes to Births Abroad, starting in 1966, where the mother's maiden name is listed too. UKHC marriage indexes, 1950-60, are in the same volumes as those registered with British High Commissions, 1961-65, and these mention the surname of the other partner in each case, as well as the place, year and folio of the registered entry. Indexes to deaths recorded by UKHC between 1950 and 1960, and by British High Commissions, 1961-65, give name, age, place of death, year, volume number and reference to the entry itself. The UKHC returns cover Asian and African Protectorates of the British Crown, too.

From 1966, Births Abroad, Marriages Abroad, and Deaths Abroad are in union annual indexes for each event regardless of whether they occurred on the high seas, on land or in the air.

Ionian Islands, 1818-64

The indexes to military registers of births, deaths and marriages in the Ionian Islands extend over the years 1818-1864. The handwritten entries give name, island, volume and page, but not the year, a pattern followed by the civil register indexes, and those of the chaplains (*sic*) returns. This is not very helpful if the name you are looking for is a common one, but at least you can locate the island.

War deaths:	*Boer War 1899-1902*
	First World War 1914-1921
	Second World War 1939-1948

These are the records of men who died abroad during or immediately after the wars listed above.

Entries give the regimental number which may be necessary if you are trying to locate a First or Second World War grave through the Commonwealth War Graves Commission at Maidenhead in Berkshire, or try service records (for more about this see *Army Service Records of the First World War*).

Adoption (England and Wales)

Before January 1927 there was no central registration of adoption in this country.

Since time began childless couples have brought up unwanted children and the informal fostering of illegitimate babies within the family was a commonplace. Masters might adopt orphan apprentices and men sometimes adopted girls to rear them as suitable wives. There was normally no record of these arrangements (a mention might appear in the adopter's will) but you might find records relating to parish adoptions, or those by private charities. Parish Overseers of the Poor and Poor Law Union Boards of Guardians might arrange for adoptions for children who would otherwise have been a burden on the rate payers. There may be evidence of such adoptions among parochial or Poor Law Union material in county record offices.

In the last century the numbers of poor orphan children grew and orphanages proliferated, many under the auspices of religious bodies; the best known are Dr Barnardo's, the Church of England Children's Society (originally the Waifs and Strays Society), the National Children's Home (Methodists). The Roman Catholic Church also ran a number. Specific searches may be conducted by these organisations for a fee. By 1900 there were in the region of twenty adoption agencies. Informal adoption of poor children by middle class couples seems to have become popular during and after the First World War when a war baby-boom coincided with a drop in the birth rate among the middle and upper classes. In 1926 legislation was introduced for the control of adoption and a registry set up. Private arrangements still continued, however.

Adoption indexes and certificates from 1927 at the FRC

In the ONS/FRC you can consult the indexes to the Adopted Children Register which was opened in January 1927. They are bound in red and buff with a yellow spine and are kept in the area shown on the plan. The indexes are arranged chronologically and alphabetically by the name of the adopted child and you can order the certificate of adoption in the same way as you order a birth certificate, but using a different form.

Adoption certificates *refer only to the adoptive parents and the child's adopted name; there is no reference to the child's natural parents or his/her original name.* The child's exact birth date is given and the country of birth only (pre-1959). The date of adoption is noted and the name of the authority making the order. From 1959 the registration district of birth is given if the child was born in England or Wales and the country of birth if he/she was born elsewhere.

Finding out who the natural parents were

There are two ways of making the link with the child's original birth certificate, which gives his/her original name, the name of the mother (and father if entered), and an address.

1. **If you are the adopted person** you can apply to the Adoptions Section of the ONS under section 51 of the Adoption Act 1976. If you were adopted before 12 November 1975, then the law requires you to see a counsellor before you can be given the information to enable you to obtain your original birth record. If you were adopted after 1976 there is no legal necessity to see a counsellor. Write to the ONS at the following address:

Adoptions Section
Office for National Statistics
The General Register Office
Smedley Hydro
Southport
Merseyside PR8 2HH
tel: 0151 471 4831

You could subsequently contact NORCAP (the National Organisation for Counselling Adoptees and their Parents). The latter is a charity which may be able to offer assistance to people wanting to trace their relatives. NORCAP's address is:

112 Church Road
Wheatley
Oxfordshire OX33 1LU
tel: 01865 875000

2.   Under section 50(5) of the Adoption Act 1976 application may be made to the courts for the Registrar General to divulge the link between the record of the adoption and the original birth record. Such applications are very rare and generally only succeed on medical or inheritance grounds.

You can ask for your name and address to be recorded in The Adoption Contact Register. Part I of the Register is for adopted persons and Part II lists birth parents and other relatives of an adopted person. The Registrar General will send to the adopted person the name of such relatives, together with their given addresses when a link is made between an entry in Part I and Part II. The Registrar General will inform the relations that this has been done. No details about the adopted person can be supplied to a birth parent or relative. Registration fees are payable for entry in the Register. Application forms may be obtained from the Adoptions Section, The Registrar General, Office for National Statistics, at the Southport address given above.

The Scottish Link

In the past those with Scottish ancestors simply had to go to Scotland to chase them up. This is no longer the case. Records relating to Scottish forebears are still in Scotland, but there is a computerised index search facility in the ONS/FRC which may save you having to go there or, at least, provide you with enough preliminary information before you make a trip.

First buy one of the guides to Scottish genealogy from the bookshop. The most useful guide is probably Cecil Sinclair's *Tracing your Scottish Ancestors* (HMSO, revised edition, 1997.

Now go to the Scottish Link area on the ground floor.

The ONS/FRC has an on-line link to the computerised indexes held at New Register House in Edinburgh. The terminals are situated at the far side of the public search room, facing you as you go in (see plan). For a fee (currently £4 per half hour, but the fee will be reviewed in the near future) you can search the database. It is advisable to book before you visit. Telephone 0171 533 6438 to make a booking. You can book a computer terminal for up to two hours.

The indexes cover:

Births, marriages and deaths 1855 to date

Adoption registers from 1930. As with adoption records for England and Wales (*see* p 35 ff) the indexes are only to the adopted name and the records themselves provide no details of natural parents or original birth name. To make the link with the registration of birth apply to the General Register Office for Scotland at New Register House (address below). The entries are merged into the computerised index of birth registrations.

Divorce files 1 May 1984 to date. You can search this under surname, forename and year, and the screen will then display the other spouse's surname, date of the marriage, divorce year, court and serial number. Earlier divorce decrees granted by the Court of Session were noted on the marriage entry itself.

Old parish registers 1553-1854. (Established Church of Scotland only so are far from comprehensive): You can search the index by county and decade, and for all Scotland.

1891 census returns. A name index gives name, age and sex, county and registration district of residence. You can make a county, registration district or all Scotland search. To get the full information as to the rest of the family, household members, occupations and place of birth, you will need to order a copy of the enumerator's entry from the film at New Register House.

Copies of the records themselves can be ordered (for a further fee) from the General Register Office for Scotland at New Register House, 3 West Register Street, Edinburgh EH1 3YT. Ask for a form at the enquiry desk in the Scottish Link area. You will have to post it off yourself with the fee enclosed.

1881 census returns; this index is available at the FRC. Its format is the same as the index for England and Wales (as reproduced on p 107) and the 'on-line' version available as part of the Scottish Link makes it possible to ***bring up on the computer screen at the FRC all the information on the original returns***. At the touch of a key or two there are about 4,000,000 souls, with all their details. No real need to order copies from Edinburgh for this one!

Earlier censuses (from 1841) can be researched at New Register House. Wills (sixteenth century to the 1970s), registers of land holding and other records are held by the Scottish

Record Office at General Register House, Princes Street, Edinburgh EH1 3YY, tel: 0131 535 1314.

The Society of Genealogists has indexes to Scottish Commissariat wills, 1514-1800.

The service records of Scotsmen in the British Army can be researched at PRO Kew (*see* the companion guide to this volume, *New to Kew?* and *Army Service Records of the First World War*).

The GRO(S) has also recently launched a new service on the Internet, 'ORIGINS', providing online access to their indexes.

If you cannot come to the FRC yourself

As explained on p 22 you can consult the indexes to births, marriages and deaths in England and Wales locally and then send for certificates. It is advisable to make a booking at the library where the fiche indexes are held. You should be aware that the GRO references of entries before 1993 are of no use when ordering certificates from local register offices, and also that the registration district names in some of the older indexes may have changed as district, have amalgamated, split or altered their boundaries.

Alternatively you can order certificates by post, fax, phone or e-mail from the ONS, if you have the necessary details. Ring 0151 471 4800 for further information. There is a priority service for those in a hurry. The e-mail address is http://www.ons.gov.uk/.

For foreign 'events' you will have to write to the ONS at the address on p 22.

If you want to employ a professional researcher you can find one from among one of the many who advertise in family history magazines. Be wary - cheapest is not necessarily best.

PART III
The Public Record Office Search Area

Family Records Centre - First Floor

Plan of the PRO search area

1   Meetings room
2   Exhibition - Introduction to Family History
3   Information and Advice
4   Microfilm Reader Printers
5   Census Reference Area: Census finding aids; IGI
       Finding Aids Microfiche
6   Registers of Wills, Estate Duty,
       Nonconformists and Miscellaneous Births
       Marriages and Deaths Indexes;
       Family Search; Library and Maps
7   Census, Wills, Estate Duty,
       Nonconformist and
       Miscellaneous Births,
       Marriages and Deaths
       Microfilms; Surname
       Indexes, including
       1881 Census
       Surname
       Indexes
8   Male
       Toilets
9   Female
       Toilets
10   Disabled Toilets

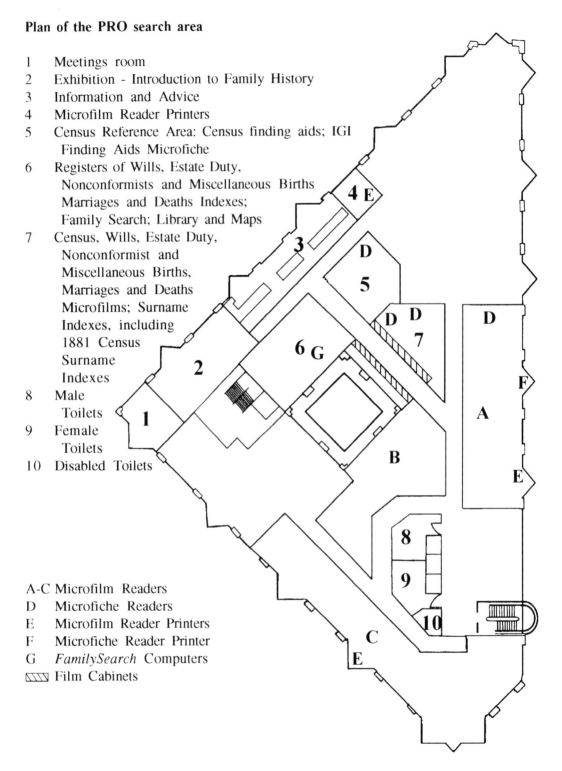

A-C Microfilm Readers
D   Microfiche Readers
E   Microfilm Reader Printers
F   Microfiche Reader Printer
G   *FamilySearch* Computers
◺◺◺ Film Cabinets

The Records

No original records are kept in the PRO search area. The records you can search on film/fiche are:

Census 19th century

Wills medieval to 1858 (Prerogative Court of Canterbury only. These can also be read at PRO Kew)

Death Duty Registers 1796 to 1857 (registers 1858 to 1903 can be read at PRO Kew)

Nonconformist Registers mainly c.1775-1837

Miscellaneous Registers of births, marriages and deaths of British citizens abroad 1627 -1960 (see also the ONS series of foreign register indexes downstairs)

It may take you a bit of time to find your way round the records and if you are raring to go you might like to dip straight into the name indexes (on fiche carousels in the middle of the research area) or the CD-ROM program *FamilySearch* (on the terminals). These will give names and data about many millions of individuals spanning three hundred years. For the fiche indexes you need to know the county where your ancestors were (you could, of course, check them all), but with the CD-ROM you can go straight in there with names and approximate dates!

The main name indexes are:

the **name index to the 1881 census of England, Wales, Channel Islands and Isle of Man**; fiche arranged by county, except for the latter two. A consolidated index will soon be available.

the **IGI** for Great Britain; the LDS index to parish register (mainly baptismal) entries and data submitted by members, 16th to 19th century. Fiche arranged by county.

FamilySearch **CD-ROM**. A computerised later edition (plus addenda) of the above, plus Ancestral File, made up of family pedigrees submitted by LDS church members and others.

See pages 48-51 for more about these indexes.

How the system works

In the PRO's search area you will find:

Research Enquiry Desk: ask here first for *FamilySearch*

a reference area with census catalogues, census street indexes, 1992 IGI on microfiche, some London directories

areas A, B & C: microfilm readers for census, photocopying points (DIY)

area A:
>   census, wills, administrations, Death Duty registers, nonconformist registers, indexes to miscellaneous foreign births, marriages and deaths films in cabinets, microfiche of 1891 census in cabinets

>   microfiche readers, census surname indexes, including 1881 Census Surname Indexes on microfiche

area G:
>   *FamilySearch* computers

>   calendars for wills, administrations, lists for Death Duty registers, nonconformists registers, indexes to miscellaneous foreign births, marriages and deaths

>   catalogues and sundry indexes of wills at the FRC and elsewhere, marriage licence allegations and bonds, some London parish register transcripts

>   a small library of reference books, maps and county directories

Census Reference Area: a photocopying counter

Microfiche readers for the 1992 IGI

Microfilm Reader Printers

The first desk you come to is Reception.

- If you want to look at the census, wills, administrations, Death Duty registers, nonconformist registers or indexes to miscellaneous foreign births, marriages and deaths, collect a numbered black box from the shelves in the census reference area. This corresponds to your seat/microfilm reader number. Find your seat in areas A, B or C.

- Calendars for wills, administrations, lists for Death Duty registers, nonconformist registers, indexes to miscellaneous foreign births, marriages and deaths can be consulted in the General Reference area.

- If you only intend to consult the fiche indexes you can choose any free microfiche reader. Use the orange card as a marker for the fiche you remove from the fiche carousels.

- If you want to use the CD-ROM go to the research enquiry desk to obtain a *FamilySearch* pack. You can use the CD-ROM for up to an hour without restriction. After this, if there is a waiting list, you may be asked to let someone else have a go.

All the sources are on film or fiche and since it is a help-yourself system there is no delay.

Turn to the relevant pages of this guide to find out how to find the film/fiche you want. You help yourself to the film/fiche, putting the numbered dummy box or orange card in the place of the film/fiche.

Buying copies

There are a number of reader/printers where you can make your own copies. You buy a card at the photocopy desk to operate them.

If you don't fancy doing this, you can get the staff to do it for you. When you have identified the pages you want copied on the film, take the film to the photocopy counter. Make sure you note the page and folio numbers which you want copied before you take the film off the reader.

Should you want to order photographs or high quality colour copies, note the reference and ask the staff at the counter how to proceed.

Researching the records

Using the 1881 census name index

Let us suppose you have made a start with your family tree using the indexes in the ONS on the ground floor and have taken the data from the certificates you have bought (this has probably taken a few weeks). You might easily have identified some ancestors who were born by 1881 - maybe your own grandparents or great-grandparents. If you have a rough idea where they lived (which county) go to the 1881 name index of that county and you should be able to find them straightaway.

This remarkable research tool lists everyone who was in England, Wales, the Channel Islands and the Isle of Man on census night, 3 April 1881 - 25,974,000 souls.

There are two sets of the indexes on fiche on the carousels in area A, arranged alphabetically by name within counties; London and Middlesex are together.

First find a microfiche reader and take the numbered card from it. Remove the fiche you want from the carousel and put the numbered card in the pouch in its place.

The fiche will tell you a good deal about your chosen ancestor - where he/she was born, age, current address, occupation and relationship to the named head of the household. The columns headed: 'Piece RG 11/' 'folio no' and 'page no' gives the PRO reference to the census return itself. A sample page of the fiche is illustrated on page 107.

Now go and get the microfilmed census returns from the cabinet (as explained on p 55), wind on until you get to the folio and page number given, and you will see the whole family or household unit laid out for you (see example opposite). Or you can consult the 'As Enumerated' fiche on the carousels next to the name index fiche, using the 'RG 11' reference number and 'folio no' to identify the correct fiche.

Using the LDS indexes

You may be able to use the LDS indexes to get your family back to their pre-central registration roots. The CD-ROM will also help you to find out what research may have been done on your family already, by members of the Church.

*A page from the 1881 census return for Wharton Street, Clerkenwell, East London.
(RG 11/349 f 95 p 33)*

The International Genealogical Index (IGI)

This is an index of many millions of names taken from prime genealogical sources all over the world and made available on fiche. For Britain this means primarily baptism and marriage entries in parish registers. There are more baptisms than marriages, because a single marriage might produce many offspring. The IGI is of prime use for locating families before central registration started in 1837.

The index is arranged by county and looks like this:

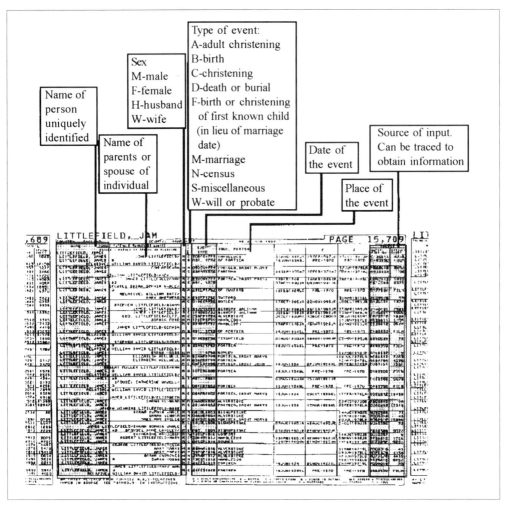

The International Genealogical Index (IGI)
(reproduced by kind permission of the Church of Jesus Christ of Latter-Day Saints)

Find a fiche reader and take the appropriate fiche from the carousels in the census reference area, using the numbered card to mark the place.

Not all parish registers are included. You will find a microfiche list of which ones are in the fiche pouches; it is called 'Parish and vital records listings', and is a separate set of fiche on the carousels.

Use this in conjunction with *The Phillimore Atlas and Index of Parish Registers* (a copy is in the library or you can buy it in the shop) to work out what the IGI covers for your area. Remember that in the eighteenth and nineteenth century many of our forebears were nonconformists. All the PRO's authenticated nonconformist registers (which can be read on microfilm in Areas A, B or C, *see* p 89) are indexed on the IGI. Some parish registers have only been ***partially included*** - watch out for this, it can cause problems.

Not all the entries on the index are extracted from parish register films direct, some have been submitted as 'compiled records' by members of the Church. You will be able to identify these from the 'source column' (they are not prefixed by the letters CAM or P). They have not been independently verified, so are unauthenticated and should be treated with caution.

The index is a most useful working tool for the genealogist for the pre-1837 period; people moved around in the past much more frequently than is generally supposed so you can utilise the index to track down migrants.

Pitfalls:

> There may be ***errors and omissions*** - once you have found out where the family were, ***check the parish registers themselves.*** You can find out where these are by consulting *The Phillimore Atlas* (cited above) and telephoning the local record office concerned (listed in J Gibson and P Peskett's *Record Offices and Where to find Them* in the library). *The Atlas* will tell you if there is a transcript which you can pop over to the Society of Genealogists to consult.

> Not all the information from original documents appears in the index, so always back-check the records themselves.

> The ***'unauthenticated' entries*** (referred to above) may be spurious or unreliable.

> Some counties have rather ***thin coverage.***

The **arrangement of names is phonetic**; beware of missing your name altogether:

Cain	see Cane
.	
.	
.	
Cane	
Kane	Albert
Cain	Amos
Kayne	Ann
Cain	Anne

This is a sensible arrangement as names in the past were often spelt in different ways.

Your family may **not be in the same county** where you found them on a certificate or in a census return. Try the CD-ROM version (*see* below) which transcends county boundaries. If there is no terminal available immediately, search the fiche for the adjoining counties.

The IGI is updated every few years. The FRC has the 1992 fiche edition for Great Britain only; the 1993 IGI for the British Isles and the rest of the world can be consulted on the CD-ROM (see below).

You can inspect the 1988 IGI, covering the world at the PRO, Kew, on microfiche. There is a separate bound 'parish and vital records listing' to this.

The *FamilySearch* CD-ROM

***FamilySearch* is most useful for locating families before central registration was introduced in 1837.**

There are ten terminals in the library area where you can consult the CD-ROM.

FamilySearch has the 1993 edition of the IGI (see above) and an addendum produced in 1994. It is no respecter of county boundaries and you can ask it (for instance):

What Albert Coxes have you got baptised round about 1822?

Who were the children of Augustus and Emily Simpson born in the 1730s?

Have you got a marriage between Treacher and Ross in the 1650s?

Apart from the IGI, *FamilySearch* also has data from Ancestral File (information about families and individuals submitted to the LDS by its members) and the Family History Library Catalog in Salt Lake City.

FamilySearch has millions of names and facts which can be brought together to provide direct information about individuals. Tap in what you know about your ancestor and you never know what you will find! But make sure you don't fall into the trap of thinking that it is a comprehensive database.

Copies of the very clear laminated instruction leaflet are available by the terminals.

The IGI is widely available in record offices and libraries. *FamilySearch* can be used at LDS Family History Centres and some local libraries.

FamilySearch contains fewer entries from parish registers on the IGI than earlier editions. Those for 1984 and 1988 are probably the most informative.

The census returns 1841-1891

The Victorian census returns are the single most fruitful group of records for family historians in this country. They list almost everybody in England and Wales, the Channel Islands and the Isle of Man on:

6 June	**1841**
30 March	**1851**
7 April	**1861**
2 April	**1871**
3 April	**1881**
5 April	**1891**

You can research the returns for England and Wales and the offshore islands in the PRO's research area on the first floor; the Scottish census returns for 1881 and 1891 are indexed on the *Scottish Link* program which you can use in the ONS research area on the ground floor (see p 38). Indexes to the surviving Irish censuses are available in some LDS Family History Centres and the returns themselves are in Dublin and Belfast (see pp 13-14).

There are copies of census films in many local record offices and libraries; they are listed in J Gibson and E Hampson's *Census Returns 1841-1891 on Microform: a directory to local holdings* (Federation of Family History Societies, 6th ed. 1994, reprinted 1997), available in the shop and in the census library.

Before you start your research

You will need an address in a large town or city, or the name of the town, village or hamlet and county (except for the 1881 census, see above p 46) because the censuses are arranged by place. There are name indexes, but they are variable in quality, and not every place is covered. There are also street indexes for many of the big towns and cities to help you find a specific address in each census.

To help you understand the records and find what you want, buy Susan Lumas' *Making use of the Census* (PRO Publications, 3rd ed. 1997). In the census research area there are laminated instruction sheets giving guidance on each decadal census to 1891.

Access to the census area

On entering the PRO's research area collect a numbered black box from the shelves in the census reference area. This has a number on it corresponding to the number of your seat/microfilm reader. Find your seat and go to the census reference area.

Name indexes to the censuses

The 1881 microfiche county name indexes are comprehensive and excellent (described on p 46); they are available on fiche in area A.

There are also name indexes of various sorts compiled by family history societies for 1841, 1851, 1861, 1871 and 1891. These are listed by place and county, so you will need to know roughly where your family was. Some are just lists of surnames. They are kept in folders in cabinets in the reference area, or are available on a fiche carousel just along from the cabinets. Each folder tells you if the contents are now elsewhere. Each entry gives a census film reference, folio and page number, which you should write down.

Take the reference (such as HO 107/100/23) from the name index. Help yourself to the film from the cabinet.

Using directories to find your family in the census

One way of getting an address for city dwellers is by using printed street directories. There are London directories for each year after census year in reference area A and the library. More complete sets can be consulted in the nearby London Metropolitan Archives or the Guildhall Library.

Using a birth, marriage or death certificate to find an address

A simple way of finding your family in the census returns is by taking an address from a birth, marriage or death certificate (see pp 26-27).

Don't be surprised if your family are not at the address you have got from a certificate - our ancestors moved around more than you might think, especially poor city dwellers, 'moonlighting' from one lodging to another.

Finding a census entry

You need to know where your family was living when the census was taken (unless you are researching the 1881 census). The name of the

our ancestors moved around more than you think

village will do if they were country folk. If you know, or suspect, the Archer family were living in Ambridge in the mid-nineteenth century, you can quite quickly go through the Ambridge returns. If, however, the Archers were living in London, it would be a very long task to find them without knowing the area and preferably the street.

Finding your census film reference: villages and small towns

Once you have got an address, you need to find the registration district number for your place in the place-name indexes, then the microfilm number from the reference books (which are arranged sequentially by registration district numbers for 1851-91, and by page number for 1841) in the reference area and then help yourself to the appropriate film from the cabinets in area A.

Look at the books labelled *Place Name Index* for the census year you are researching. The indexes are colour coded:

    1841 green
    1851 red
    1861 blue
    1871 brown
    1881 yellow
    1891 black

Each place has a number which is highlighted in yellow. Note the yellow number and find it in the book labelled *Reference Book,* where it is also coloured yellow. For 1841 **only** the number appears at the bottom of each page. Later numbers are sequentially listed by district.

Note the 'class code' number in the top left hand column of the *Reference Book* for your census (eg RG 12) and the 'piece number' below it (2311 etc. in the example opposite). You will need a three-part reference (such as RG 12/2311) to find the film you need, except for 1841 when the reference is four-part.

The class codes are as follows:

    1841 HO 107
    1851 HO 107
    1861 RG 9
    1871 RG 10
    1881 RG 11
    1891 RG 12

Reference			RG 12
RG 12	Registration District	Registration Sub-District	Civil Parish, Township or Place
		WORCESTERSHIRE	
2311	376.KIDDERMINSTER [Street Indexed]	1 Chaddesley	Chaddesley Corbett Stone Shenstone Rushock
2312		2 Wolverley	Broom Churchill Wolverley Broadwaters Cookley
2313		3A Kidderminster	Kidderminster Borough(4)
2314		3B "	"
2315		3C "	"
2316		3D "	" Kidderminster Foreign (3)(4) Franche Wribbenhall
2317		4 Lower Mitton	Lower Mitton (8)
2318		5 Bewdley	Bewdley Dowles (Salop) Ribbesford Upper Arley (Staffs)
2319	377.TENBURY	1 Tenbury	Burford (Salop) (4) Boraston (Salop) Watmore (Salop) Nash (Salop) Tilsop (Salop) Weston (Salop)

A page from the 1891 census Reference Book.

Finding your census microfilm

Armed with your three-part reference number, take your numbered black box from the side of your reader and go in search of the cabinet which contains your film (in area A).

When you find the film, put the black box in its place, take the film back to your seat and put it onto the reader, following the instructions on the sheet at the end of each row. You may prefer to read the 1891 census on microfiche. These too are in area A with the other fiche sets.

You are now ready to start your research!

Finding your census film reference: cities and large towns

Consult the lists of street indexes for your census year; the lists are on the shelves below the *Place Name Indexes* and *Reference Books* for each census. The lists will tell you if there is a street index for a particular part of London, or for your town. The *Reference Books* also indicate street index numbers. Look at the 'street index' column on the right of each page for these. This is important because some suburbs of large towns are included in the street index, but do not appear in the prepared accompanying lists. If your family lived in a provincial town you will now need to look your street up in the books labelled *Country Street Indexes*, which are in the same bookcase. Find the volume with the corresponding street index number written on the spine. If your family lived in London, there is a list of these too, and the number of the appropriate street index can also be found in the *Place Name Indexes* and *Reference Books*, since the lists may exclude parts of London which are actually covered. It is probably best to consult the *Place Name Indexes* first. Once you have located the street index number, look for it in the volumes of *London Street Indexes* in the same bookcase. The index numbers are marked on the spine.

If you cannot find a particular street in London, try *Book 90, London Streets and their localities*, found on the shelves for each census year, which is an alpha-

Name.	Postal District.	Locality.	Parish.	Year.
Wharves (The)	S.E.	River-side . .	. East Greenwich .	
Wharves .The)	W.	Uxbridge-road .	. Hammersmith .	
Wharncliffe-street .	E.	Bonner-street .	. Bethnal-green .	1860
Wharton-place .	E.	School-house-lane	. Ratcliff .	
Wharton-road .	W.	Sinclair-gardens.	. Hammersmith .	
Wharton-street .	E.C.	King's-cross-road	. Clerkenwell .	
Whateley-road .	S.E.	Kent-house-road	. Beckenham .	
Whateley-road .	S.E.	Lordship-lane :	. Camberwell .	
Whatman-road .	S.E.	Brockley-road .	. Lewisham .	1887
Wheathill-road .	S.E.	Croydon-road .	. Penge .	1867
Wheatley's-cottages	S.E.	Ravensbourne-street .	Greenwich .	
Wheatsheaf alley .	S.W.	Bishop's-road .	. Fulham .	
Wheatsheaf-lane . .	S.W.	South Lambeth-road .	Lambeth .	
Wheatsheaf lane .	S.W.	Upper Tooting .	. Streatham .	
Wheatsheaf-whf.-alley	E.C.	Upper Thames-street.	City . .	

Book 90

betical listing, showing their locality and parish, enabling you to find them by looking for the larger area. *Book 91* and *Book 92* list alterations to and abolished street names within the London County Council area up to the year of publication in 1912. This is to be found on the shelves next to the 1871 finding aids and in the library.

Another avenue may be to look at one of the contemporary London directories, on the shelves next to the 1871 finding aids, which will show street intersections, or to consult a map of the area. If you are working from an address on a certificate from the ONS (ground floor) the name of the registration district will be given on the certificate.

The entry for your street will have four parts eg RG 9/450/31. The class code and piece number (eg RG 9/450) indicates which film you should take from the cabinet. The last number is the folio number which will help you find your street on the film.

If you cannot find a place in the census Place Name Indexes

Try looking at the *Hamlet Index*, found in the bookcase next to the 1871 finding aids and in the library. This shows the place each hamlet was included with, the county, and the registration district.

For Wales, the index *List of Parishes in England and Wales*, 1897, also in the library, and the binder containing a *Welsh Place Name Index* for the counties of Brecon, Denbigh, Flint, Glamorgan and Monmouth, at the Enquiry Desk, may be helpful, otherwise you may have to resort to one of the maps held at the same Desk.

Finding your census film and your place on the film

Take your numbered black box and the reference number you have got from the indexes to the microfilm cabinets in area A and find the cabinet which contains your film. Put the black box in the place of the film and return to your seat. Put the film on the reader, following the instructions displayed. Find the folio number (stamped on the top right hand corner of every other page of the returns).

The 1841 indexes give a book number as well which is shown on every frame of the film as part of the reference strip. It appears also on the title page of each book (as left).

PLACE	HOUSES		NAMES of each Person who abode therein the preceding Night.	AGE and SEX		PROFESSION, TRADE, EMPLOYMENT, or of INDEPENDENT MEANS.	Where Born	
	Uninhabited or Building	Inhabited		Males	Females		Whether Born in same County	Whether Born in Scotland, Ireland, or Foreign Parts.
Upper W Linton St 24		1	Thos H Cooper	25		School Master	Y	
			Ann Do		20		Y	
			Susan Do		20		Y	
			William Boggis	30		Warehousem	N	
			Mary Do		36		N	
			Ann Bell		20	Dom M	Y	
25		1	Charles Hodgson	30		Printer	N	
			Dorothy Do		30		N	
			Charles Do	1			N	
			Margaret Do		13 dau		Y	
			Sarah Wynn		45	Nurse	Y	
			Mary Lait		6	F S	Y	
			Eliza Do		15	F S	Y	
26		1	Edmund Seymour	40		Clerk	Y	
			Mary Do		25		Y	
			Caroline Bathe		20	F S	Y	
27		1	Thos Cufsons	35		Merchant	N	
			Hannah Do		30		N	
			Charles Do	2			Y	
			Emma Blackford		25	F S	Y	
28		1	Cath Plowman		30		Y	
			Do Do		13		Y	
			Frances Do		11		Y	
			Francis Do	5			Y	
			Henrietta Do		4		Y	
TOTAL in Page 18	5			7	18	215		

The 1841 census return for part of Upper Wharton Street, Clerkenwell.
(HO 107/659 book 5 f 40 p 18)

The 1861 census return for part of Fordrough Street, Birmingham. More detailed information is recorded than in 1841. (RG 9/2139 f 64 p 23)

What the census returns contain

The census is a house to house survey and the entries list everyone 'at home' on census night, including those doing night work. Visitors and servants were included. People described as 'servants' may be what we call apprentices. Members of the family who were absent, perhaps staying with relatives, at school, or working away will appear in the lists for the households or institutions where they were on census night. The inmates of institutions are listed, workhouses, boarding schools, hospitals, lunatic asylums, reformatories and men in barracks, on barges on inland waterways, on board Naval ships in home waters and on British merchant vessels. Where there were more than a hundred people in an institution there is a separate set of schedules under the town where they were, indicated in the *Reference Book* by a bracketed number after the name of the place.

Naval and merchant shipping returns rarely survive before 1861.

From 1851 the returns give names, ages (not always reliable), the relationship of each person to the head of the household, sex, marital status, occupation, parish and county of birth and whether blind, deaf or dumb. From 1871 imbeciles, idiots and lunatics are noted.

The 1841 census was less informative. Adult ages are rounded off to the nearest five below. Instead of giving the place of birth, the entries are classified as follows:

YOUR AGE?
"Oh, just turned seventeen, if you please, sir."
PUZZLE—FIND THE CAT.

Ages given in census returns are not to be relied upon. Census puzzle, 1891. (COPY 1/94 f.19).

'Y'   born in the county of current residence
'N'   not born in the county of current residence
'S'   born in Scotland
'I'   born in Ireland
'F'   born in foreign parts (non-British subjects)

At the end of each family household the enumerator drew a line - / through the vertical column to the left of the names; at the end of all the households in the building he drew two lines thus - //.

Maps

You may have problems following the census enumerator's route and knowing where you are on the census, especially if there are no street indexes. Maps can be very useful; there is a miscellaneous collection in the library. 25" Ordnance Survey maps show the exact location of houses.

If you are researching the London census it may be worth your while going over to the nearby London Metropolitan Archives to consult the maps there. You could have a look in its photograph collection and see if there is a picture of the street your Victorian ancestors lived in.

There are also two series of maps in the library which give the boundaries of the registration districts, sub-districts and the civil parishes. One set, correct for the years 1851 to 1861, is not complete, as some of the maps do not survive. The other is a complete set for 1891 (for both see the class list for RG 18). Note your registration district number when using the 1891 set since that is the way the maps are arranged within the counties. Some of the maps are available on microfiche. Ask at the Enquiry Desk about these.

These maps are most useful when an individual large house or a tiny hamlet cannot be found in street indexes or other finding aids. Once the place is located on the map the parish containing it can be determined by noting the place name which has a pink line through it within the thin red boundary line. Then note the sub-district by observing the pink boundaries within which the place falls, and the large pink spot on the place which gives its name to the sub-district. Finally, note the green boundary lines and the green spot on the place which is the name of the registration district, and return to the lists and indexes for the year you wish to research.

Problems and Solutions

1. *You cannot find your village in the Place Name Index*

    Your place may be a hamlet or small place included in another. Look in the *List of Parishes in England and Wales*, 1897. It will tell you in which parish it is included.

2. *You cannot cope with the microfilm/fiche reader*

    Follow the instructions on the leaflet at the end of each table. If that doesn't work watch carefully what your neighbour is doing. Ask.

3. *Your family are not at the address you have for them*

    Your family has probably moved on. People moved around a great deal more than you might think.

    Perhaps they never lived at the address on the certificate at all - as we have seen, addresses on marriage certificates are notoriously unreliable.

    The street may have been renumbered. For London you can check in the *LCC List of Streets and Places*, *Book 91* and *Book 92*, 1912 (labelled as *Alterations and Abolished Street Names in London*) These can be found with the directories next to the 1871 finding aids bookcase, and in the library. Number changes are included in two volumes in the library.

4   *You cannot find your street in the London street indexes*

    Perhaps the street was in the process of being built and the houses there are identified by the name of the terrace. There are various London guides (including *London Terracd Streets 1841-1881*, in the library) which can help you sort this out.

    There is a list of all the London streets for which no 1861 census returns survive. Ask at the Enquiry Desk about this.

5   *You cannot read the film/fiche*

    If you really cannot read the film or fiche, even with the magnification on the reader at its maximum, you might try nabbing a seasoned researcher. Family historians share a great conspiracy of co-operation and if you appear friendly, but quietly desperate, there is always a kindly soul who will come to the rescue.

    The staff will help you out with the odd word, but remember there are several hundred of you and only a few of them. Take a copy of the entry and puzzle over it at home.

    If the film is really unreadable, you may be allowed to see the original. You will have to go to PRO Kew for this. Ask.

6. *You don't understand the description of your great-great-grandfather's occupation*

Occupations can be a problem. Try consulting the following in the library: *Census of England and Wales 1881, Instructions to the Clerks Employed in Classifying the Occupations and Ages of the People.* This is kept at the Enquiry Desk.

Using the census to find out where your family was before central registration started in 1837

One of the easiest ways of locating your family pre-1837 is by taking the place of birth from one of the earlier censuses.

The 1851 census is probably the best; there are name indexes and there is a fair chance that at least some of the family enumerated in 1851 will have been born before registration started. Once you have a place of birth for one of the family, you can then go to the IGI on the fiche carousels or The *FamilySearch* CD-ROM (*see* p 50) and look for his or her baptism.

Censuses before 1841 and after 1891

Censuses were taken from 1801 but, until 1841, they were head counts only. A few lists of names survive from the 1801-1831 surveys; but it is well worth checking. These lists are deposited locally; see J Gibson and M Medlycott, *Local Census Listings 1522-1930* (FFHS, 3rd ed. 1997) in the library.

Details about ages and birthplaces of people from the 1901 census may only be given with their written consent, or that of a direct descendant or next-of-kin, and on payment of a fee (£40 at the time of writing). Ask for an application form from the Enquiry Desk. You must supply an exact address and the name you expect to find there.

Photocopies

You can make your own copies using one of the reader/printers. Buy a token from the photocopy counter. There are clear instructions by the machines but ask if you get stuck.

If you want the staff to make the copies for you, take the rewound film to the photocopy counter.

You will need to supply an exact reference to the **page and folio number**, taken from the census film.

Giving up altogether

Don't be surprised if you get frustrated and confused at your first foray into the census. Historical research is not straightforward - that is half the fun of course. What about going and having a good old English meal at one of the local pubs or restaurants and coming back refreshed?

giving up on the census

The PRO staff will do a census search for you for £18.80 (at the time of writing). Ask for an application form and details.

For more extensive exploration of the records you can get a list of names of independent professional researchers. Ask at the desk.

If the census has not yielded up its riches to you - perhaps you are fed up chasing your family round the countryside and never finding them - why not try some other records? You could go downstairs and do some digging in the birth, marriage and death indexes or have a go at the wills and Death Duty Registers in the general reference area. Try not to thrash around wildly after people of the same name, but stay focused on the people and places you know about, and, of course, dates, otherwise you could well end up researching someone else's ancestry for them, but not your own.

Wills and Administrations

You can research indexes to pre-1858 wills (some), lists of nonconformist registers (some), on microfilm and Death Duty records from 1796, together with the list of indexes of miscellaneous births, deaths and marriages of Britons abroad. You can also look at FamilySearch CD-ROMs on one of the ten computer terminals. Ask at the Enquiry Desk for an information pack.

You will need to collect a numbered black box from the shelves in the census reference area when you come in. The number on the black box is your seat/microfilm reader number in areas A, B or C.

Prerogative Court of Canterbury (PCC) wills and grants of administration

PCC wills can be read at the FRC or at PRO Kew. If you are going to Kew it is better to read them there where related probate records are kept (see Jane Cox, **New to Kew?,** *PRO, 1997).*

Before you start your will search you could buy Miriam Scott, **Prerogative Court of Canterbury Wills and other Probate Records** *(PRO Reader's Guide no. 15, 1997) from the shop. This is a useful step by step guide to the PCC will and administration records at the FRC.*

Are all English and Welsh wills in the FRC?

No. Officially registered wills are distributed thus:

Wills proved from 12 January 1858:

in District Probate Registries (locally proved wills only).

in Somerset House (Principal Probate Registry; copies of **all** wills proved in England and Wales). The public search room of the PPR is due to be relocated in June 1998 to First Avenue House, 42-49 High Holborn, London WC1V 6HA. Check before visiting. It is open to all from 10 am to 4.30 pm, Monday to Friday. For a small fee you can read a will and order a copy. Postal enquiries, which are normally dealt with within 21 days, should be addressed to The Chief Clerk, York Probate Sub-Registry, Duncombe Place, York YO1 2EA, tel: 01904-671564.

Microfiche copies of indexes to wills and administration grants, 1858-1943, can be inspected at the Centre. Help yourself to a microfiche card and substitute it for each microfiche you remove from the cabinet.

Wills proved before January 1858:

in the FRC (some)
in local record offices (some)

Before 1858 there were hundreds of probate courts, most of them church courts, with the addition of some peculiars, which lay outside the jurisdiction of the local bishop.

The ruling as regards jurisdiction of the courts was that anyone who died with goods and cash (not real estate; see p 80) to the value of £5 (£10 in London) in more than one diocese had to have their will dealt with by the archbishop's court. This ruling ceased to be strictly observed and by the 1830s the Prerogative Court of Canterbury was handling one third of all the country's probate business, including many very small estates. Thus one might expect to find the will of a seventeenth or eighteenth-century yeoman farmer proved in a minor court (and now in a local record office).

The wills in the PRO (FRC) are those which were 'proved' ie given the official stamp of authority by the most senior court in the south of England, the Prerogative Court of the Archbishop of Canterbury (PCC). PCC wills go back to 1383. Most of the early ones are those of rich and titled people; the later ones come from all ranks of society.

English and Welsh people who died abroad (if they had personal estate at home) had their wills proved in the PCC or church court of the diocese where it was held. You will also find the wills of many ordinary soldiers and sailors in the PCC.

Wills of people of small means tended to go to minor courts and are now in county record offices. There are indexes to some of these on the shelves in the wills area and you can also use the Death Duty indexes from 1796 to 1903 to locate them (see pp 80 ff). Use J Gibson's *Probate Jurisdictions: Where to Look for Wills* (FFHS, 4th ed. 1994, updated 1997) to find out where locally deposited wills are kept and what indexes there are. There is a copy in the library and you can buy it in the shop.

Many wills, indexes and lists have been filmed and you can order the records to read in your local LDS Family History Centre.

Note for the period 1653-1660 there was a single civil probate court run by the officers of the PCC. The records are with those of the PCC and the published will/administration indexes for this time (on the shelves in the general reference area) provide a country-wide index which is very good for locating 'lost' ancestors. Bear in mind, however, that many people did not bother with grants of probate or administration during the Interregnum, when it was a matter of dealing with a London-based registry rather than just going to the local court.

What are the chances of finding a will for your ancestor in the PRO/FRC?

The richer he was, the more likely it is that you will be successful in your search. Nevertheless, there are many thousands of PCC wills for quite humble people, especially in the nineteenth century.

There are more southerners than northerners.

If your rich ancestor lived in the north of England, unless he had investments, goods or property in the south, his will would probably have been proved in the court of the Archbishop of York (Prerogative Court of York) whose records are in the Borthwick Institute of Historical Research, St Anthony's Hall, Peasholme Green, York YO1 2PW; tel: 01904 642315.

Did your ancestor leave a will at all?

Before the present century only a very small percentage of the population left wills which went to probate, perhaps as little as 5% of the male population.

Far fewer women than men left wills; the property of married women was usually disposed of by their husbands and spinsters might be too poor to bother with any formal disposition. However single women's wills, once found, can be very informative for the family historian.

Grants of administration

In some cases if a man died without leaving a will ('intestate') the court would make a grant of administration to his next-of-kin.

Usually these grants were only made if:

- the widow or next-of-kin thought someone else might make a claim on the estate.

- there was some need for legal title to be established. One of most usual circumstances was that someone who was owed money by the deceased applied to administer his estate - that being the surest way of a creditor getting his hands on what was owed him!

The main records of PCC grants of administration are brief entries in a series of registers called 'Administration Act Books'(reference PROB 6) which you can see on film at the FRC. Special grants are entered at length (EAL) in series of registers called 'Act Books: Limited Administrations' (PROB 7, PRO Kew) from 1810. Before that date they are in PROB 6, at the end of each section.

See p 74 for a description of how they are indexed and what information they contain.

There are laminated leaflets about pre-1700 and post-1700 wills and grants of administration close to the general reference area.

How to find a will at the FRC

(Remember you can also research these wills at PRO Kew)

All registered copies of wills are on film; the class code for them is PROB 11. You will need an approximate date of death. The numbers given in the will indexes refer to 16-page gatherings (quires) in the will registers; they are *not* page or folio numbers.

1383-1700

There is a laminated leaflet about pre-1700 wills near the general reference area.

Consult the volumes of printed indexes on the shelves. The volumes up to 1700, which are listed in Miriam Scott's book (cited above) are also available in good reference libraries. Note the year of probate and the number given by the entry. This is the gathering or quire number.

Take the black binder labelled PROB 11 from the shelves and find the part of the list which refers to your probate year and the gathering or quire number. It might, for example, be PROB 11/56 and the quire number be 34.

Make a note of the reference PROB 11/56. Go to the film cabinets in area A and help yourself to the film numbered PROB 11/56, putting your numbered black box in its place.

Put the film on your reader and wind it on until you find number 34. The gathering/quire number appears in large figures at the top right corner, every 16 pages. The will you are looking for is entered somewhere on the 16 pages following the page marked with the number. The name is written in the margin.

Ignore the stamped or manuscript numbers which appear on every frame.

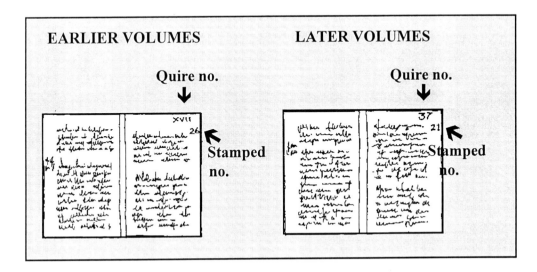

1701-1749

There is a laminated leaflet about post-1700 wills near the general reference area.

For these years there is a typescript consolidated index on the shelves in the general reference area, compiled by the Friends of the PRO. Proceed as above.

1750-1800

For these years use the printed index volumes edited for the Society of Genealogists by Anthony Camp, also on the shelves. Proceed as above.

1800-1852

Consult the yearly manuscript indexes labelled PROB 12. They are not in strict alphabetical order, so you may, have to go through all the 'R's, for example, to find the will of a person beginning with R such as John Richardson. The indexes give the county of death, not the exact place. 'Pts' means the person died abroad (Parts). North Britain is Scotland.

The indexes to 1664, 1701-49 and 1800-52 are both to wills and grants of administration; make sure you have the right sort of grant. There are headings to guide you and, for the most part, administration entries have a month by them and no number.

Find your person, note the year of probate and the number by the entry and proceed as above.

1853-1858

There is a printed union index to wills, also on the shelves. This is also on microfiche, with the indexes of later wills up to 1943, in the main search room.

Buying a copy of the will

Wills can be long and complicated and very instructive, so you will want a copy of your will to take home and ponder over. Take it to a reader/printer and make your own copy. Alternatively, take the rewound film to the photocopy desk and get them to do it for you. In this case, you will need to note the **stamped number** on every frame.

Understanding the will

Wills may be complex documents using unfamiliar archaic and legal terms. There is a glossary in Miriam Scott's book (cited above).

Some of the very early wills are in Latin and you may need to consult dictionaries which you will find in the library.

The staff will help if you have difficulty with the odd word. If you are at a loss with the whole thing, you can get the name of a palaeography specialist from the Enquiry Desk. He/she will charge a fee to transcribe and/or explain it to you.

Most wills begin 'In the name of God Amen' *(In Dei Nomine Amen)*. If you find something which starts *Memorandum quod* it is a nuncupative or spoken will. If you come across something on the film which is a long Latin entry, it will probably be a 'sentence' (verdict) in a law suit.

The Latin clause at the end of the will up to 1733 is called the 'probate'. All you need to take from this is probably the name of the executor, the relationship to the deceased, if stated, and the date.

There are some important considerations you should bear in mind:

- landed property was often disposed of by other means than wills ie by marriage or other settlement.

- children might have their inheritance settled on them at marriage or at twenty-one - so not all children are necessarily mentioned in the will.

- wills could take a long time to be proved, years sometimes, so search the indexes several years forward from the death date. Straightforward wills were usually proved within a few months of death.

Reading the original will

The will which you can see on film at the FRC is a court copy. If you want to look at the original document, written (usually) in the handwriting of your ancestor's lawyer (or his clerk) and signed by the man himself, then you can do so at PRO Kew (in class PROB 10). You will have to give five days' notice as they are stored out of the building.

Original wills tend to be easier to read than the court copies. Errors in transcription are very rare indeed. The seals which many of the original documents carry are not usually the testator's own seal; they are much more likely to be the seals of the attorneys responsible for drafting them.

Registered copy will of John Jacob Vesenbeck (original overleaf). (PROB 11/635 s 23)

In the Nasme off God Amen

I find my selff perfectle in all my senses so I leave to my son Johan Jacob Vesenbeck Peruikmaker off Mosbach in the Palat, inal one schilling and cut hem off for ever to recive ane thing I belonget to me or mine for hes extream wikednes to me ——

I likweise leave a schilling to my thaughter Anna Kunigunda Vesenbeckin I thont know haer Married nahme then sche has vari much contributet to hes comeng hier and never shal ßite to me for all sche has recivet much more from me then haer Mother had ——
my joungest thakter Susanna Margretha Langfrizin I leave 2 doo —— guineas and in case my Wife and haar 2 sons Jacob and Edward Vesenbeck diet without legitimal issue then all Wal es left devolves to haar or haar legitimal issue evere thing Wat ther is Wich for one persohn will be considerable ————

                                          a shilling bod I leave
my son Jacob Vesenbeck I leave all my Workin implements all my patrons off brimston all my baß and glaß and evere thing Wat belongs off making the seals I likweiß leave hem my diamant Ring Wich I haff off Mr Ladvoval for 10 pound off hes Mother schould be death haar clohts and Hadcloß the linen and all Wal es left I my selff being death also, elfe evere thing belongs to me, NB the rich Rooth and Wiß silk cloathe belongs to Jacob, and jou may agree amonst Jou to give James Jones a suit off black kloths off hes mother to change a suit for hem and because my wife often expresses haar selff off she has Edward in haar keepeng he schould schut so shmall as a mouse, and I have experient haar
                                                          haar

Original will of John Jacob Vesenbeck, a German seal maker. (PROB 10/1736)

Limited probate

If the indexes show that a limited grant was made you should look at the entry in the Limited Probate Act Book (PROB 9, PRO Kew) as well as the will.

You have read the will - are there any other records which relate to it?

For many PCC wills there are supporting documents of one sort and another at PRO Kew, especially probate inventories, listing household items, cash, debts, stock, crops and animals, with an approximate valuation for each.

Death Duty Registers (from 1796) may add a good deal (*see* pp 79 ff) since they are kept open for fifty years.

If there was a lawsuit over the estate there may be a whole range of documentation, *see* below.

Records of lawsuits

If the will indexes show that the will was proved 'by sentence' or 'by decree' (abbreviated to 'sent' and 'decr') it means that there was a fight over the estate and you may be able to find out a great deal more about your ancestors in the records at PRO Kew than is to be gleaned from the will alone.

The PCC was very thorough in its proceedings and numbers of witnesses might be called to give evidence in a case, servants, relatives, friends. You may get the whole village turning up in court.

Some wills were 'propounded' (proved by witnesses) and there may be surviving documentation of this procedure. The will indexes will not necessarily indicate this.

The only sure and certain way of checking that there was a suit or propounding is to search the fairly complete series of Acts of Court Books (PROB 29, 1536-1819, integral indexes) and the loose Acts of Court (PROB 30, 1740-1858, in monthly bundles, alphabetically by the name of the deceased). This may be a lengthy business and there are various short cuts to finding surviving records. It should be stressed, however, that the Acts of Court are the only complete record of litigation/propounding.

Disputes handled by the PCC are about the authenticity of wills not the contents. The PCC might have to decide whether or not a man was sober and/or sane when he dictated his will. If the family decided it was not fair that he had left all his money to the local Quaker meeting, then, unless their lawyer advised them to claim he was not of 'sound and disposing mind', they would have to go to the king's court. Probate cases more often than not went to the equity court of Chancery which had jurisdiction over trusts and real estate. Chancery records can be researched at PRO Kew and are described in the companion volume to this, *New to Kew?*

How to find a grant of administration

Records of intestacy grants are on film (for the most part) and you can help yourself to the films from the cabinets labelled PROB 6 in area A. They can also be read at PRO Kew.

The grants are indexed with the wills in the yearly manuscript indexes (PROB 12); for the period 1559-1664 (1661 incomplete) and 1701-1749 there are published indexes (listed in Miriam Scott's book, cited above). All are on the shelves in the general reference area. The Society of Genealogists has a card index for the period 1750-1800 which they will search for a fee.

Having found your man in the index, note the year, month and county of the entry and turn to the binder labelled PROB 6. Find the three-part reference for the Act Book for the year in which your grant was made. You need this three-part reference, such as PROB 6/6, to identify the film.

Take a numbered dummy box from the signed shelves, and place it in the cabinet when you help yourself to the film. Wind on until you find your entry. The entries are arranged by month before 1744, but there are subsections within each month, so make sure you check all through.

From 1744 the Act Books are arranged in five divisions called 'seats'. Four of them are county sections. Section three, for instance, contains grants for intestates who **died** (not lived) in Derbyshire, Gloucestershire and eleven other counties. The first section (the 'Registrar's Seat') should always be checked as it contains, amongst other things, all grants made following litigation and thus relates to people who lived all over the country.

The seat arrangement is given below:

Bedford	4	Norfolk	4
Berkshire	4	Northampton	3
Bristol	2 & 3	North Britain	1
Buckinghamshire	4	Northumberland	1

Cambridgeshire	4	Nottingham	1
Carlisle	1	Oxford	3
Chester	1	P.T.S. (Abroad)	1
City of London	5	Rutlandshire	3
Cornwall	2	Shropshire	3
Cumberland	1	Sunderland	2
Derbyshire	3	Somersetshire	2
Devonshire	2	Southampton	2
Dorsetshire	2	Staffordshire	3
Durham	1	Suffolk	4
Essex	4	Surrey	2
Gloucestershire	3	Sussex	2
Herefordshire	3	Wales	3
Hertfordshire	4	Warwickshire	3
Huntingdonshire	4	Wiltshire	2
Ireland	1	Worcestershire	3
Kent	1	York (The County and entire province)	1
Lancashire	1		
Leicestershire	3	Grants on Litigated Estates (by decree)	1
Lincolnshire	4		
London	5	Outlying London Parishes (Middlesex)	4
Middlesex	4 & 5		

Understanding the grant

The wording of the grant follows a pattern and, even though they are in Latin before 1733, it is simple to extract the information you want.

The name in the margin is that of the dead man. The first thing noted in the body of the entry is the date, then follows the name of the grantee (wife, next-of-kin or creditor), then his/her relationship to the deceased and the latter's address.

From 1796 the value of the personal estate is given in the margin.

A sample is given overleaf.

Note limited grants (appearing as *limitat*) are entered in full in separate registers from 1810 (PROB 7). These can only be read at PRO Kew; there is a short note of them in the ordinary Administration Act Book (PROB 6).

Richus Swifte ad de bonis commis'mensis Martii 1617	Decimo quarto die emanavit comissio Francisce Swift relte Richi Swift nuper parochie beate Marie Magdalene in Barmondsey Com Surr' des' hentes etc. ad administranda bona iura et credita dci des' de bene etc. in persona Richi Goodall notarii publici procuris sui etc. iurat'	Winton Ascensio in Inventarium exhibitum xxj Blasii Computavit
Richard Swifte admon of goods unadministered granted March 1617/8	On the fourteenth day [of March] a commission issued to Frances Swift the relict of Richard Swifte of the parish of the Blessed Mary Magdalene in Bermondsey in the county of Surrey deceased having etc [whilst he lived and at the time of his death goods etc. sufficient to found the jurisdiction of the Prerogative Court] to administer the goods rights and credits of the said deceased she being sworn truly to administer in the person of her proctor, Richard Goodall, notary public	Winchester diocese Inventory to be exhibited by Ascension; exhibited on [March] 21st Account to be returned by the feast of St Blaise (3 February); [administrator] has accounted

Entry in Administration Act Book, 1598/9 (PROB 6/6, f.9). The left-hand marginal note indicates that a 'de bonis' grant was made nineteen years after the original grant. Richard Swifte's widow had evidently died without administering her husband's estate.

Problems and Solutions

1. *There is not much information in the Act Book entry - is there anything to supplement it?*

    There may be an inventory (list of possessions) or a bond. These records are kept at PRO Kew.

    Death Duty Registers can be very useful in supplying extra data (see pp 80 ff) for the periods they cover (1796-1903, on film to 1857 at the Centre). Later registers are held off site and take five days to be produced at PRO, Kew. Indexes to 1903 are on microfilm at the Centre.

    Like wills, intestate estates might be the subject of litigation (*see* above p 73 for possible sources). The most common sort of suits were 'interest causes', disputes as to who was related in what way to the deceased. It was not uncommon for women to claim marriage to wealthy men to try and get their hands on the money.

2. *There is an administration in the indexes for my ancestor but I cannot find it on the PROB 6 film - why not?*

    Either you are looking in the wrong 'seat' (*see* p 74) or your grant is 'special' or 'limited' (restricted in some way).

3. *My will/administration search has been unsuccessful - what shall I do now?*

    There are three main reasons why you have not found a will/administration:

    *   You have not searched for a long enough period - probate could drag on, sometimes for years. Keep looking.

    *   The grant was not made in the PCC but in the Prerogative Court of York (PCY) or one of the minor courts. If this is so, you will have to go elsewhere to read the will or grant, but while you are in the FRC there are several things you can do to help you on your way.

    *   No grant was ever made - very common. There is nothing to be done in this case.

To find out where you have to go to read locally proved wills/administrations, consult J Gibson's *Probate Jurisdictions, Where to Look for Wills* in the library or buy it in the shop. This also reveals details of printed indexes which you may find on the general reference area shelves (*see* above).

Look at the indexes to the Death Duty Registers in the film cabinets labelled IR 27; the catalogue is on the shelves in the general reference area. *See* p 80 for an explanation of how these provide a country-wide probate index. There is a laminated leaflet nearby explaining the registers and indexes.

Look at the Death Duty Register entry for your local grant; in the case of an administration it will probably tell you more than the locally held grant itself.

Death Duty Records

These records, which complement and supplement English and Welsh wills and administrations (granted in some cases where no will was left, explained on p 67) can be read at PRO Kew or the FRC depending on the year and type of register you require:

- 1796-1857 at the FRC (except Reversionary and Succession Registers, *see* p 83).

- 1858-1903 at PRO Kew (give five days' notice when ordering these records as they are kept off site).

- Indexes for the whole period are on microfilm at both the FRC *and* PRO Kew.

The Death Duty records are one of the most important genealogical sources in the PRO. Approximately 9,000 registers and their indexes document the levying of a series of different duties and provide:

- a countrywide probate index (not comprehensive) for the period 1796-1858. This is vital for dioceses such as Exeter where the local records have been destroyed.

- information about many thousands of families, their wealth, possessions and landed property which often supplements what is found in wills and administrations.

Death Duty records are one of the most useful genealogical sources
in the PRO, but you may need help to interpret them

Using the Death Duty indexes as a country-wide probate index

As explained on p 66 there were many probate courts before 1858 and there is no central index to them.

One way of finding an ancestor's will/administration is by checking through the films of the Death Duty indexes (IR 27) at the FRC or at Kew. These indexes are by no means comprehensive but they do cover a good many estates.

The registers record the levying of a series of different taxes. Legacy Duty was introduced in 1796 and was payable on legacies of £20 or more and residues of personal estate left by will or intestates. Inheritance by near relatives was exempt (*see* below). Further enactments: the Legacy Duty Act of 1805 and the Stamp Act of 1815 extended the duty liability to near relatives and also to cover legacies and residues which were raised by the sale of real (freehold) estate as directed in a will. Succession Duty (1853) became payable on all gratuitous acquisitions of property at death, personal and real. Probate Duty was introduced in 1881 (a tax on all personal property passing at death) and Estate Duty in 1894 (payable on all property transfers at death).

1796-1815

Only a small percentage of estates were dutiable during this period, so the indexes are slim and the chances of finding a particular individual rather remote. The Duty, at this stage, was limited to legacies and residues left to people who were *not* close relatives. Thus wills which benefited only wives, children, parents and grandparents will not appear at all. Between 1805 and 1814 legacies to wives and children were exempt from duty, and from 1815 onwards spousal gifts only.

1815-1858

For this period there is far wider coverage. In 1854 there was said to be a Death Duty entry for one of every sixteen people who died in the country.

Very small estates were not dutiable.

Finding your way round the indexes (IR 27)

Consult the binder labelled IR 27 in the general reference area. You will see that the 605 volumes are in various series (*Note* for the period 1796-1811 there is a strictly alphabetical index on the bookshelves and you will not have to bother with the filmed indexes):

- Prerogative Court of Canterbury (PCC) wills 1796-1811
- PCC administrations 1896-1857
- Country courts wills and administrations 1796-1811
- Country court administrations 1812-1857
- PCC and country court wills 1812-1858
- Court of Probate wills 1858-1881
- Court of Probate administrations 1858-1863*
- Court of Probate wills and administrations 1882-1903.

   * There is a gap in the administration series 1864-1881.

For the period 1812-1903 note the film you need (eg IR 27/339) and take it from the cabinet in area A. Wind on the film until you find your ancestor's name; the arrangement is ***not strictly alphabetical***, though a code of the first three letters is used, so all surnames beginning 'TRO....', for example, are grouped together. Note the court where the grant was made (fourth column), the register number (fifth column) and the folio number (sixth column).

A page from the index to the Court of Probate wills for 1861. (IR 27/339)

Having noted the name of the court where the grant was made, you will be able to find out where to read the will/administration. The courts are referred to by abbreviation: PY for Prerogative Court of York, Archd. for archdeaconry court, Const. for bishop's consistory court. Use J Gibson's *Probate Jurisdictions, Where to look for Wills* in the library to find out what courts there were and which record office now has the wills. If the fourth column of the index says PC, then the registered will is in the FRC (see p 66) or PRO, Kew.

The year and folio number are your way into the Death Duty Registers themselves.

Using the Death Duty Registers to supplement information in wills/grants of administrations

The entries in the registers may add considerably to what you have found out in the will or administration (admon). (*Note:* you will not find a Death Duty entry if no will was proved or grant of administration made by a court. Many people did not bother with any formalities after a death and just shared out the assets among themselves in an amicable way). Entries relating to intestate estates may be especially useful as beneficiaries may be listed with addresses and other information about them, perhaps spanning several generations as the revenue officers chased up individuals. Dates of death, sale proceeds, and married names will build up a more detailed picture than the will itself.

Legacy Duty was paid on a sliding scale according to the relationship of the beneficiary to the deceased; the relationship is noted in an abbreviation (*see* key) in the 'consanguinity' column. This information is particularly useful for identifying illegitimate children and clarifying the exact relationships of individuals to the deceased.

The total valuations should be treated with caution; they were valuations made before the deduction of debts and expenses and, before 1853, took no account of any real estate unless it was to be sold to pay legacies or go into the residual estate (*see* probate glossary). After 1853 there is information about descent of landed property outside the will.

The Reversionary Registers (only to be seen at PRO Kew) are particularly informative as they concern trusts set up in wills which were administered over a long period; as each transfer of property took place Succession Duty was payable and entries may span several generations in a family, supplying details of marriage, death and change of address. You will know that there is a Reversionary Register entry as the entry in the main register will be annotated **RR.**

The Duties and the coverage of the registers

There are five series of registers:

- Registers recording Legacy Duty, 1796-1893

- Registers recording Succession Duty 1853-1893 (Probate Duty from 1881)

- Registers recording Estate Duty 1894-1903 (incorporating the two other taxes)

- Succession Arrears Registers, opened in 1885 and 1889 to cope with outstanding claims for duty for the periods 1853-1865 and 1866-1878 respectively

- Reversionary registers, created in 1899 to deal with outstanding claims from 1812-1852.

All registers from 1858 and the Reversionary and Succession Registers are only available at PRO Kew (give five days' notice to read them).

The indexes to all the registers are the IR 27 series described above.

The registers are arranged thus:

PCC wills	1796-1811	IR 26/1-178
PCC administrations	1796-1857	IR 26/179-286
Country court wills and administrations	1796-1811	IR 25/287-437
Country court administrations	1812-1857	IR 26/438-534
Will registers (all courts)	1812-1881	IR 26/534-3292 (items from 2086 onwards at PRO Kew only)
Intestate registers (admons Principal Probate Registry)	1858-1881	IR 26/3293-3433
Will and administration registers (Principal Probate Registry)	1882-1894	IR 26/3434-4855
Reversionary Registers	1812-1852	IR 26/4856-4867
Succession Registers	1853-1894	IR 26/4868-6262
Succession Arrears	1853-1894	IR 26/6263-6282
Estate Duty Registers	1894-1903	IR 26/6283-8687

Approximately 500 Estate Duty Registers and eleven Succession Duty Registers are missing.

The gradual extension of taxes (*see* p 80) means that you have more and more chance of finding your ancestor's estate as the years pass. The Board of Stamps, which administered the taxes, did not usually bother to pursue collection unless the assets were valued at £1,500 or more, so many of the entries may just be a total valuation without any further detail.

If you find the annotation 'Upper Limit', it means that your ancestor was worth over £1,000,000 (under the 1815 Stamp Act such estates were exempt).

Finding an entry in a Death Duty Register

Use the indexes on film (IR 27) as described on p 81 or the typescript indexes if you are researching the period 1796-1811.

Note the folio number given in the indexes and go to the catalogue labelled IR 26 on the bookshelves. Find the reference number for the register which contains your folio for the right year. Remember the registers are in different series as listed on p 83 and that IR 26 numbers from no. 2086 refer to volumes which can only be read at PRO Kew.

Help yourself to the IR 26 film found in the cabinets in area A and find the folio number which you took from the index. Now your problems start - what on earth does it all mean?

The sample reproduced on p 86 and the key below will help you to sort the entry out, but Death Duty Registers can be complicated. It is essential to take a copy. You may need professional advice. Ask at the enquiry desk and they will give you the name of an independent professional researcher who will help you to understand the entry, for a fee. There is also a laminated leaflet to help unravel the terminology and abbreviations in the registered entries.

Key to Death Duty Registers

Consanguinity

BF	=	brother of a father (uncle)
BM	=	brother of a mother (uncle)
Child)	=	child of deceased (legitimate)
Ch)		
DB	=	descendant of a brother (niece, nephew, etc)
DS	=	descendant of a sister (niece, nephew, etc)
DBF	=	descendant of a brother of a father (ie cousin)
DBM	=	descendant of a brother of a mother (ie cousin)

DSF	=	descendant of a sister of a father (ie cousin)
DSM	=	descendant of a sister of a mother (ie cousin)
DBGF	=	descendant of a brother of a grandfather
DMGM	=	descendant of a brother of a grandmother
DSGF	=	descendant of a sister of a grandfather
DSGM	=	descendant of a sister of a grandmother
G child	=	grandchild
GG child	=	great-grandchild
G daughter	=	grand-daughter
G son	=	grand-son
SF	=	sister of a father (ie aunt)
SM	=	sister of a mother (ie aunt)
Str)		
Stra)	=	stranger in blood
Strag)		
Stra BL	=	stranger, brother-in-law
Stra DL	=	stranger, daughter-in-law
Stra NC	=	stranger, natural child (ie illegitimate)
Stra ND	=	stranger, natural daughter (ie illegitimate)
Stra NS	=	stranger, natural son (ie illegitimate)
Stra NC (of a daughter)	=	stranger, illegitimate child of a daughter
Stra NC (of a son)	=	stranger, illegitimate child of a son
Stra (sent)	=	stranger, servant of deceased
Stra SL	=	stranger, sister-in-law or stranger, son-in-law
Stra or 'son'	=	stranger, natural son (ie illegitimate)
Stra or 'daughter'	=	stranger, natural daughter (ie illegitimate)

What deemed

abs	=	absolute legacy, ie unconditional
abs & int	=	absolute and interest
abswp	=	absolute legacy with a proviso (conditional legacy)
anny	=	annuity
annywp	=	annuity with a proviso (conditional legacy)
dwp	=	ditto (usually absolute) with proviso
in deft of appt eq'y am'g them	=	in default of appointment equally amongst them

A typical death duty register entry. (IR 26/1103 f 339)

339

and Profession

Where and when proved. Sworn under. £100

Eastcheap Court York
17th April 1826 Bucks

Cash received.

Name	Upon what contingency or if in Succession of equal Rate	What deemed	Amount of Annuity.	Value of Annuities and Bequests brought forward.	Rate of Duty	Total Amount of Duty.	Alterations.	Date.	Annuity Instalments. 1st Year.	Date.	2d Year.	Date.	Annuity Instalments. 3d Year.	Date.	4th Year.	Total Duty.
		Ah.	10	20	1	4		1827								4
		do	10	20	1	4										4
		Annry	10	42 120 7	1	1 5 0		1827								1 5 0
			10	37 137 3	2 1	1 7 5										1 7 5
			16	108 122 118 7	1	1 4 5										1 6 5

Death Duty records from 1903

The PRO does not have any Death Duty records after 1903 but if you are a direct descendant of the subject of your enquiry, it is possible that the Capital Taxes Office might be prepared to release some information to you. Write to The Capital Taxes Office, Ferrers House, PO Box 38, Castle Meadow Road, Nottingham NG2 1BB (tel: 0115 874 0000).

Nonconformist Registers before 1837

The FRC has filmed copies of about 6,000 authenticated registers from Nonconformist chapels. They are classified as RG 4 and may be read in areas A, B or C. They mostly cover the period 1775-1837. Those in RG 4 are indexed on the IGI (see p 48).

A much smaller collection of registers (classified as RG 8) can be read at PRO Kew. They are unindexed. See the companion volume to this guide, *New to Kew?*

Other (and later) registers may be found in local record offices or with the congregation.

About one quarter of the population are thought to have been protestant Nonconformists in the mid-nineteenth century. Your Welsh ancestors are more than likely to have been 'chapel'. The registers are a vital source for births/baptisms and burials for a large percentage of the population before central registration started in 1837. Marriages were conducted in chapels before 1754. After that, until 1837, they had, by law, to be performed in Anglican churches (except for Quakers and Jews).

From the mid-sixteenth century there were numerous groups of people who formed themselves into congregations which worshipped outside the Church of England and pockets who remained with the old religion, Roman Catholicism, notably in Lancashire. Most of the Nonconformist sects were more extreme in their protestantism than Anglicans.

If your ancestors belonged to any of these groups, Congregationalists/Independents, Presbyterians, Baptists (called collectively The Old Dissent), Methodists/Wesleyans, Moravians, Huguenots, Countess of Huntingdon's Connection and the rest, then their vital records before 1837 are the baptisms/births and burials in the chapel registers. Marriages can be found before 1754 only (except in Quaker registers); after that date the law directed that dissenters should marry in parish churches.

Nonconformists might have their own separate burial grounds. The registers of a few of these are at PRO Kew (*see New to Kew?* under Cemetery Records) and some are at the FRC (*see* p 93).

How to find your Nonconformist ancestors in the FRC

You may know that your family were Methodists or Presbyterians: you may suspect that they were as there as no baptisms or burials for them appear in the registers of the parish church.

First go over to the microfiche carousels and look at the IGI (fiche index, described on p 48) for your county. This includes the entries in the FRC's collection of Nonconformist registers (though not those in RG 8 at PRO Kew). If you don't know which county the family were in, try searching on the *FamilySearch* CD-ROM (described on p 50), but remember there are entries in the 1992 microfiche edition, which have been removed and do not feature in 1993 or later computerised addenda.

If you find your family, you should now check in the registers themselves. The reference number that you need to get your film is on the IGI eg RG 4/88. Help yourself to the film from the cabinets in area A.

If you know the name of the chapel where your ancestors worshipped, or the area they lived in, you may wish to go straight to the RG 4 catalogue, without bothering with the IGI. It is arranged by county and is in a black binder on the general reference shelves.

Why are there no registers for my chapel/area in the catalogue labelled RG 4?

- Some registers are in the class RG 8 at PRO Kew. Check the binder labelled RG 8. You will have to go to Kew to look at the records.

- Some registers are still with the congregation, or in a local record office, listed in *British Archives: A Guide to Archive Resources in the United Kingdom*, ed. J Foster and J Sheppard (London, 3rd ed. 1995) in the library. You can then ring the appropriate local record office from one of the pay phones in the basement.

- Your ancestors were Quakers, *see* below.

Quakers

The Religious Society of Friends was established in 1668.

The Quaker registers are at PRO Kew (RG 6). There are no indexes at Kew; you should go to Friends House, Euston Road London NW1 2BJ, tel: 0171 387 3601, where the library is open Tuesday to Friday and for a modest fee you can search the county digests up to 1837 which serve as indexes to the Quaker registers of minutes of monthly meetings. Many record births before 1668, deaths and burials, names of parents, and ages, whilst the marriage entries list everyone who witnessed the exchange of vows, relatives and Friends.

Roman Catholics

Roman Catholicism was illegal most of the time from the mid-sixteenth century until 1779. There were some secret congregations and some attached to foreign embassies and the royal court. There are only 44 Roman Catholic registers in the PRO; most have been retained by the congregations.

To find out the whereabouts of a particular register, telephone or write to the Westminster Archiepiscopal Archives at Archbishop's House, Ambrosden Avenue, London SW1 1QI, tel: 0171 938 3580. You can also consult M Gandy, *Catholic Missions and Registers, 1700-1800* (London, 6 vols, 1993), and *Catholic Parishes in England, Wales and Scotland, An Atlas*, by the same author (London, 1993), in the library.

The most useful publications of the Catholic Record Society can be consulted in the library at the Society of Genealogists, which also sells the above titles. You will have to pay a search fee if you do not belong to the Society, if you want to use the library.

Huguenots

If you have a French-sounding name you may have Huguenot ancestry, especially if the family comes from Spitalfields or Bethnal Green in the East End of London. 'Huguenot' was the nickname given to continental protestants (mainly French) who took refuge in this country in the sixteenth and seventeenth centuries. The main influx was in 1685 when some 40,000 are said to have arrived after the Revocation of the Edict of Nantes, which allowed them tolerance.

The foreigners set up their own chapels and the registers are chiefly in the RG 4 collection (*see* p 90). All of the Huguenot registers have been published by the Huguenot Society; these volumes are on the shelves in the library. The entries also appear in the IGI.

See New to Kew? under Immigrants for other possible sources.

A quick way of trying to establish which part of France your family came from is to consult the French section of the IGI which is on CD-ROM in *FamilySearch*. Kew has the worldwide edition on microfiche for 1988, together with a *Parish and Vital Records Listing* printout of places and periods covered.

There is a fine collection of material in the Huguenot Society Library in University College, Gower Street, London WC1E 6BT, tel: 0171 380 7094. It is a short bus or train ride from the FRC. You will, however, have to pay to join the Society and make an appointment to research there.

Other sources for Nonconformist ancestors

The central registry of Baptists, Independents and Presbyterians, includes births from 1716-1837 (Dr Williams's Registry). About 50,000 births of members of the above denominations were registered, from London, the provinces, and overseas. It was a voluntary system, started in 1742, and the Registry closed when civil registration began on 1 July 1837.

Indexes to the registry have the reference RG 4/4666-4676. Look at the RG 4 catalogue covering Middlesex in the general reference area and find the bound indexes you need on the adjacent shelves. The microfilmed registered copies themselves are at RG 4/4658-4665.

The Metropolitan Wesleyan Methodist Registry covers births from 1773-1838 (Paternoster Row). About 10,000 Methodist births were registered here after it was opened in 1818.

The index (RG 4/4680) is next to those for Dr Williams's Registry, and the registers (RG 4/4658-4665) are in the cabinets in area A.

The records of three cemeteries are also in RG 4:

> Bunhill Fields Burial Ground, City Road, London, 1713-1854 (RG 4/3974-4001, 4288-4291 and 4633. Indexes at RG 4/4652-4657)

> South London Burial Ground, East Street, Walworth, London, 1819-1837 (RG 4/4362)

> Necropolis Burial Ground in Everton, Liverpool (all denominations; RG 4/3121).

Two invaluable guides to the records and history of Nonconformity are:-

> David Shorney, *Protestant Nonconformity and Roman Catholicism, A guide to sources in the Public Record Office*, PRO Reader's Guide no. 13 (PRO, 1996). You can consult this in the library or buy it in the shop.

> Don Steel, *National Index of Parish Registers, vol 2: Sources for Nonconformist Genealogy and Family History* (Society of Genealogists, Chichester, 1973/1980). You can consult this in the library.

If your ancestors belonged to one of the denominations concerned you will find the following booklets useful (you can buy them in the shop):-

> *My Ancestors were English Presbyterians/Unitarians,* Alan Ruston (SOG, 1993)

> *My Ancestors were Baptists,* G R Breed (SOG, 3rd ed. 1995)

> *My Ancestors were Congregationalists in England and Wales,* D J H Clifford (SOG, 2nd ed.1997)

> *My Ancestors were Quakers,* E H Milligan and M J Thomas (SOG, 1983)

Miscellaneous returns of births, marriages and deaths of Britons abroad

The records of births, baptisms, marriages, deaths and burials registered in British embassies and consulates are to be found in a number of series in different places: the Family Records Centre, PRO Kew, the Guildhall Library, the Society of Genealogists and elsewhere. In the FRC you can consult the name indexes on film (RG 43) to miscellaneous non-statutory foreign returns to the Registrar General. If you want to see the registers themselves you will need to go to PRO Kew, where they are listed in the binders for RG 32 - RG 36. They relate to births, marriages and deaths abroad, and on British as well as foreign ships, of British subjects and nationals of the colonies (see also below).

To find out the whereabouts of other registers, consult the *Guildhall Library Research Guide* 2: *The British Overseas* (Guildhall Library, 3rd ed., revised 1995).

British Empire and Commonwealth

Births, marriages and deaths registered in countries which were once part of the British Empire or Commonwealth are normally to be found among the archives of those countries. See T J Kemp, *International Vital Records Handbook* (3rd ed. 1995), a copy of which is in the library. Useful information is also found in *The British Overseas* (cited above). Both ONS and the PRO have an up to date list of local Registrars worldwide.

The India Office Library (British Library Oriental and India Office Collections), from August 1998 relocated to the British Library, 96 Euston Road, St Pancras, London NW1 2DB, tel: 0171 412 7873, has about a thousand volumes containing births, marriages and deaths in India between 1698 and 1947.

PART IV
Case Studies

CASE STUDIES

Here are two case studies of typical working families, the Richardsons of Brighton and the Pearces of Potterne in Wiltshire, based largely on information from the Family Records Centre. The charts demonstrate the use of sources and research method to construct a pedigree going back to the beginning of civil registration in 1837 and beyond, utilising extracts of parochial records on a computerised database (the *FamilySearch* CD-ROM) available far away from the places themselves.

1: The Brighton Line

The starting point of this search into family history is a daughter born to one John William Richardson in mid-December 1931. Her birth was not registered in the sub-district of West Brighton in Sussex until over a month later, so the birth index of the March quarter of 1932 had to be scanned as well as that covering the three months up to and including December 1931, since the registered entries are arranged by date of registration not by date of birth. The baby was born at home, and was the youngest of John's four children by Annie Pearce, his wife. The next stage was to find the date of their marriage. The date of birth of their eldest child was known, so it was logical to use that as the starting point. A search was made in the ONS marriage indexes for John and Annie's wedding, going backwards from this date. The couple were married at the Register Office in Brighton in May 1920, and the marriage certificate indicated the groom's address as being the same one where his daughter was born more than eleven years later. John was described as a fruit merchant's salesman both in 1920 and in 1931, and was twenty-three years old when he married, a year younger than his bride.

John's father, Percy George Richardson, was dead by the time of his son's marriage. Percy is described as a stoker-engineer at a brewery on his son's marriage certificate, but when John was born in 1896, further down the same street, at 13 St Mary Magdalene Street, his occupation is given as a baker journeyman. We do not know when Percy changed his job. *The Census of England and Wales 1881: Instructions to the Clerks employed in classifying the occupations and ages of the people*, held at the Public Record Office Enquiry Desk on the first floor, contains details of main occupations and associated job titles; a look under the headings 'Brewing', 'Engineers' and 'Stokers' showed that Percy was likely to have been responsible for looking after the brewing equipment.

John William Richardson was twenty-three at his marriage in 1920, so he could have been born in 1897. But in fact his birthday fell only eleven days after his wedding day, so his birth certificate was located in the quarterly index covering April up to the end of June 1896, rather than 1897.

Birth certificate of John William Richardson, 19 May 1896 (Office for National Statistics)

From family information it was believed that John's parents Percy and Alice had at least three more children, the eldest of whom was thought to have been born about 1881, and the second around 1882. However, when the quarterly marriage indexes were searched back from John William Richardson's birth registration in 1896, their wedding was found to have taken place in the summer of 1884. The marriage certificate does not give Percy's second name of George.

Marriage certificate of Percy Richardson and Alice Taylor, 30 August 1884 (Office for National Statistics)

The Richardsons of London and Brighton
Case Study 1

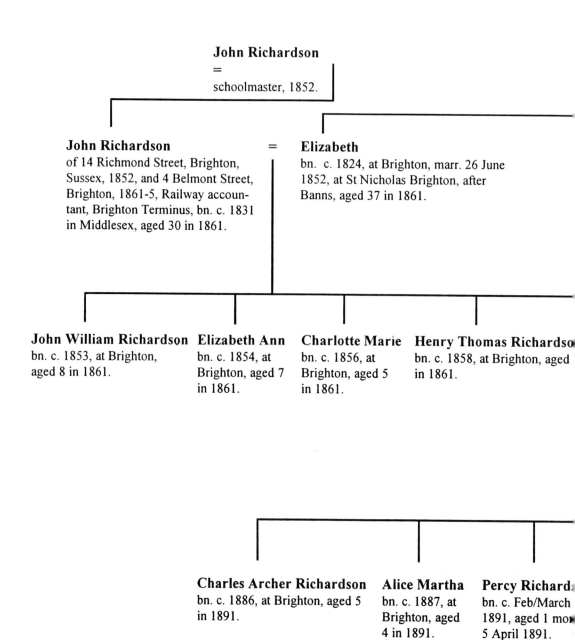

John Richardson
=
schoolmaster, 1852.

John Richardson
of 14 Richmond Street, Brighton,
Sussex, 1852, and 4 Belmont Street,
Brighton, 1861-5, Railway accountant, Brighton Terminus, bn. c. 1831
in Middlesex, aged 30 in 1861.

=

Elizabeth
bn. c. 1824, at Brighton, marr. 26 June
1852, at St Nicholas Brighton, after
Banns, aged 37 in 1861.

John William Richardson
bn. c. 1853, at Brighton,
aged 8 in 1861.

Elizabeth Ann
bn. c. 1854, at
Brighton, aged 7
in 1861.

Charlotte Marie
bn. c. 1856, at
Brighton, aged 5
in 1861.

Henry Thomas Richardso
bn. c. 1858, at Brighton, aged
in 1861.

Charles Archer Richardson
bn. c. 1886, at Brighton, aged 5
in 1891.

Alice Martha
bn. c. 1887, at
Brighton, aged
4 in 1891.

Percy Richard
bn. c. Feb/March
1891, aged 1 mo
5 April 1891.

Key:	bn.	=	born
	c.	=	circa (about)
	marr.	=	married
	↓	=	unnamed children
	QV	=	see PEARCE family tree

Thomas Pocock

=

general dealer, 1852.

Charles Taylor   =   **Phoebe Goss**

house painter, journeyman, 1863,   bn. c. 1826, at Wrotham, Kent, aged
dead by 5 April 1891.   65 in 1891, receiving parish pay.

Martha   **Percy George Richardson**   =   **Alice**   **James Pearce**   =

n. c. 1860, at   of 9 Pool Valley, Brighton, 1871   bn. 13 Feb 1863,   coal merchant,
Brighton, aged 1   and 1884, 13 St Mary Magdalene   at 23 Lomax Street,   1920.
1861.   Street, Brighton, 1891-96, baker,   Brighton, marr. 30   QV
                     journeyman 1871-96, stoker-   Aug 1884.
                     engineer at a brewery by 1920, bn.
                     6 Aug 1865, at 4 Belmont Street,
                     Brighton, dead by 8 May 1920.

John William Richardson   =   **Annie**

of 7 St Mary Magdalene   nurse (domestic), 1920,
Street, Brighton, fruit   bn. 1 Feb 1896, at Old
merchant's salesman, 1920,   Oak Lane, East Acton,
bn. 19 May 1896, at 13 St   Middlesex, marr. 8 May
Mary Magdalene Street,   1920, at the Register
Brighton.   Office, Brighton.

↓

Percy was 21 when he married, and his address was given as Pool Valley, Brighton, where he was lodging with Francis Cowley in 1881. His father, John Richardson, was dead. Alice was also 21, and a Brighton resident too. When ages are given as 21 this may merely indicate that a person was of full age, and *at least* 21, and thus did not need parental consent to marry. This can be misleading if you rely on the ages as 21 to calculate year of birth. In both cases here, however, the couple's ages were correct.

Percy George Richardson's death was not registered in England or Wales between 1895 and the September quarter of 1920, but as he was apparently born in 1865, according to his marriage certificate, he would have been 49 at the outbreak of The Great War in 1914. The indexes of Army War Deaths, Other Ranks, 1914-21, and of Naval War Deaths, Other Ranks, for the same years, produced nine entries of a Percy Richardson in the former. Unfortunately, in spite of the regiment, regimental number, rank and year of death being recorded, the index does not cite age; a reference check was made against each of these entries, giving Percy's estimated age, and name of his marriage partner, Alice Taylor, who would have been his next of kin. None of the entries matched up with the known details so it has not been possible so far to verify the date or circumstances of his death. This is a good example of the occasional stumbling-blocks you will encounter when researching family history.

Percy's birth took place at his parents' home, 4 Belmont Street, Brighton, on 6 August 1865, when he was given the second name of George. His father, John Richardson, was a Railway Accountant at Brighton Terminus; he was in all probability an employee of The London Brighton and South Coast Railway Company, founded in 1846. Staff records have been deposited in the Public Record Office at Kew (see *New to Kew?*), so it should be possible to trace his appointment, salary and career through the company ledgers, which run up to the early twentieth century.

Three generations of Richardsons were born at home, which would have been the usual pattern, but sometimes the birthplace was the maternal grandparents' house or temporary lodgings, so it is important to look at the address of the informant, normally one of the parents, to check the usual domicile of the family.

From the data gathered from the earliest birth certificate it was possible to begin looking for the wedding of John Richardson and Elizabeth Pocock, Percy's parents. It took place on 26 June 1852, at St Nicholas parish church, Brighton; John was twenty-one and Elizabeth seven years his senior. He was already working as a railway accountant and his father, John Richardson, was described as a schoolmaster. Elizabeth's father, Thomas Pocock, was a general dealer, and the two witnesses signing the register were a Thomas P and Charlotte Pocock, presumably Elizabeth's relations.

More information about the family can be gleaned from the censuses of 1891, 1881 and 1861. When the 1891 census was taken, on Sunday night of 5 April, Percy G Richardson was at 13 St Mary Magdalene Street, Brighton, with his wife and family. Because this address had been recorded on his son's birth certificate in 1896, and the Brighton census returns have a street index, it was an easy task to home in on the household. Percy, its head, was described as a journeyman baker, and had by then two sons and a daughter, aged between one month and five years of age. He gave his own age as twenty-seven and that of his wife Alice as twenty-eight, and he had a widowed boarder, sixty-five-year-old Phoebe Taylor, staying with him, receiving "parish pay" i.e. poor relief. As she bore the same surname as his wife, this suggested a family link, and Alice Taylor's birth certificate of 1863 did indeed show that her mother's name was Phoebe, formerly Goss, so she was Percy's mother-in-law. Mrs Taylor came from Kent ('Rootham' given as her place of birth in the census is probably a phonetic misspelling of Wrotham), but everyone else in the household was a native of Brighton.

The 1881 census personal name index of Sussex revealed that Percy Richardson was then seventeen, and was lodging with Francis Cowley in Brighton. Francis gave Percy's birthplace as Aldershot in Hampshire. This was inaccurate - possibly Percy's family circumstances were not well known to him. This illustrates why it is always a good idea to do as much cross-checking as possible. A look at the original enumeration showed that Mr Cowley ran a reasonably-sized bakery, employing ten resident assistants, bakers and house servants.

On 2 April 1871 the Richardson family was not listed in the census returns of Belmont Street, Brighton, where they had lived when Percy was born in 1865. In 1861, on 7 April, when the previous census was taken, John Richardson was there with his wife Elizabeth and their five young children, the eldest of whom was eight. John gave his age as thirty and his birthplace as Middlesex N.K (not known), and he was working as a railway clerk. Elizabeth was engaged as a bonnet maker, and like their offspring, was born in Brighton. Sharing the same house, though in a separate apartment, was Mary Ann Levick, an unmarried schoolmistress, apparently born at Hanwell in Middlesex fifty-eight years before, so this may be a clue to John's birthplace, since his father was a teacher too. On 30 March 1851, 14 Richmond Street, Brighton, John's address in 1852 when he married, was described as empty by the census enumerator.

This is where the Brighton Line terminates, because John Richardson travelled down there from Middlesex before 1852, probably as a recruit on the railways, and earlier branches must be tracked in the London area around 1831.

2: The Pearces come to London

Annie Pearce was twenty-four when she became John William Richardson's wife in 1920. According to her marriage certificate, she was then working as a domestic nurse and her home was in St Michael's Place, Brighton, in Sussex. Her father, James Pearce, was a coal merchant, though when Annie was born in 1896 he was described as a general labourer, living in Old Oak Lane, East Acton, Middlesex, the place of the confinement. We do not know when Annie moved to Sussex, but it may well have been in the course of her work. Annie's parents, James Pearce and Elizabeth Doe, got married at Christ Church, Chelsea, in 1891, as from 22 Flood Street. James was then twenty-eight and his bride a year younger, and both their fathers were labourers, like James himself.

The entry of the Pearce/Doe marriage in the register of Christ Church, Chelsea. It is similar to the ONS entry, but the signatures of the bride and groom appear. (London Metropolitan Archives, ref p 74/LUK/7, by courtesy of the Rector and Churchwardens)

As the 1891 census was taken four months earlier, on 5 April, this street was a good place to begin to try and discover where James was born, because his name and that of his father is not unusual and it might prove difficult to positively identify his birth entry in the quarterly indexes. Alas, neither James nore Annie were found lodging anywhere in the street or its vicinity, so number 22 might simply have been an accommodation address for them both whilst the banns were being read in the local church on the three Sundays preceding their wedding. However, a William Bridwell was at this premises, the head of a household comprising himself, his wife Amelia, and their daughter, occupying three rooms in a building which was divided up into three apartments. William was a milkman, born thirty-six years previously at Potterne, in Wiltshire, like his wife, who was the same age. One of their two lodgers also came from Potterne. As the child was born in London four years before, the family had been settled in the metropolis at least since 1887.

The 1891 census return for 22 Flood Street, Chelsea, giving the details of William Bridwell and his family. (RG 12/63 f 128v)

The Pearces of Potterne, Wiltshire, London and Brighton Case Study 2

= **Ann**
of Potterne, Wiltshire, pauper,
formerly servant, 1851, bn. c.
1774, at Devizes, Wiltshire,
aged 77 in 1851.

Mary Ann Hampton = **William Pierce/Pearce** = **Ann Underwood**

Mary Ann Hampton
bn. c. 1819, in Wiltshire,
marr. 22 Sept 1834, at
Potterne, aged 22 in 1841,
dead by 30 March 1851.

William Pierce/Pearce
of Potterne Wick, 1841, Butts
1851, 1871, and Lower Street,
1861, all in Potterne, general
labourer, 1841, thatcher 1851, bn.
c. 1811 or 1813, at Potterne, aged
28 in 1841, 38 in 1851, 50 in 1861,
60 in 1871, dead by 3 April 1881.

Ann Underwood
of Lower Street, Potterne, 1881,
1891, agricultural labourer, 186
81, bn. c. 1818-26, at Potterne,
aged 43 in 1861, 47 in 1871, 55
in 1881, 71 in 1891.

William Pearce
of Butts, Potterne,
thatcher, 1851, bn. c.
1836/7, at Potterne,
aged 4 in 1841, 15
in 1851.

Richard Pearce
of Lower Street, Potterne,
agricultural labourer, 1861,
bn. c. 1840, at Potterne, aged
10 months on 6 June 1841,
11 in 1851, 21 in 1861.

George Pearce
bn. c. 1853, at
Potterne, aged 8 in
1861.

Sarah
of Lower Street,
Potterne, agricultural
labourer, 1881, bn. c.
1857 at Potterne, aged
4 in 1861, 14 in 1871,
24 in 1881.

(Hester) Jane
bn. c. 1838, at Potterne,
aged 3 in 1841, 13 in
1851.

Thomas Pearce
of Lower Street, Potterne,
agricultural labourer,
1861, bn. c. 1842/3 at
Potterne, aged 9 in 1851.

Ann
bn. c. 1855, at Potterne,
aged 6 in 1861.

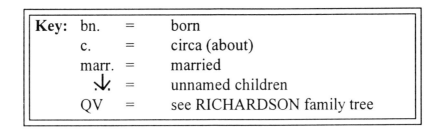

Key: bn.   =   born
      c.   =   circa (about)
      marr. =   married
      ↓   =   unnamed children
      QV   =   see RICHARDSON family tree

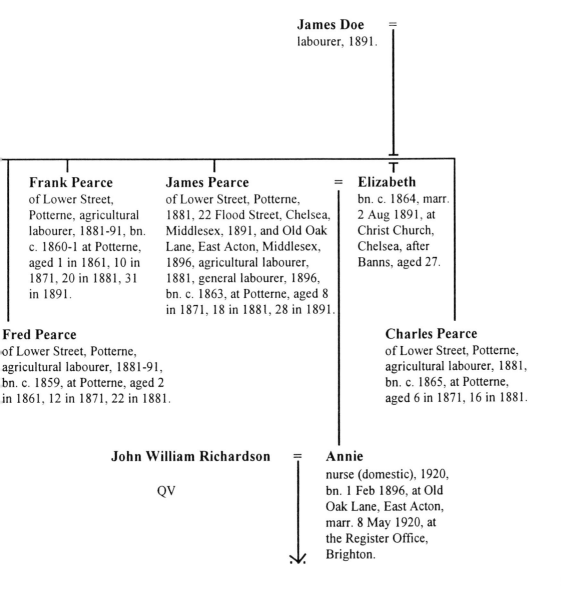

James Doe =
labourer, 1891.

Frank Pearce
of Lower Street,
Potterne, agricultural
labourer, 1881-91, bn.
c. 1860-1 at Potterne,
aged 1 in 1861, 10 in
1871, 20 in 1881, 31
in 1891.

James Pearce = **Elizabeth**
of Lower Street, Potterne,   bn. c. 1864, marr.
1881, 22 Flood Street, Chelsea, 2 Aug 1891, at
Middlesex, 1891, and Old Oak   Christ Church,
Lane, East Acton, Middlesex,   Chelsea, after
1896, agricultural labourer,   Banns, aged 27.
1881, general labourer, 1896,
bn. c. 1863, at Potterne, aged 8
in 1871, 18 in 1881, 28 in 1891.

Fred Pearce
of Lower Street, Potterne,
agricultural labourer, 1881-91,
bn. c. 1859, at Potterne, aged 2
in 1861, 12 in 1871, 22 in 1881.

Charles Pearce
of Lower Street, Potterne,
agricultural labourer, 1881,
bn. c. 1865, at Potterne,
aged 6 in 1871, 16 in 1881.

John William Richardson = **Annie**
                                 nurse (domestic), 1920,
QV   bn. 1 Feb 1896, at Old
                                 Oak Lane, East Acton,
                                 marr. 8 May 1920, at
                                 the Register Office,
↓   Brighton.

The Pearce-Doe wedding certificate of 1891 shows one of the two witnesses signing the register as a W Bridwell, who may well have been this person, and their erstwhile landlord when they arrived in London. A speculative search was made of his birthplace, Potterne, to see if James Pearce could be located there in April when the census was taken. This failed to pick up an unmarried James Pearce aged about twenty-eight, though nine separate households included Pearces among them that night, and an Ann Bridewell, a widow of fifty-three, had five sons in her house at Butts, in the same village, the only Bridewell or Bridwell (variant spellings are fairly common) household there.

A search was made in the 1881 census county personal name indexes for London, Middlesex and Wiltshire, but did not disclose any James Pearce of eighteen or thereabouts, who was a son of the household of a William Pearce in Middlesex. However, a James Pearce of that age, an unmarried agricultural labourer, was at Potterne, his birthplace, in his mother's house, and her name was Ann. No William Bridwell or Bridewell was listed under Wiltshire, of the alleged age of twenty-six.

The actual returns of Potterne for the night of 3 April 1881 gave Ann's address as Lower Street. She was herself an ag. lab. (agricultural labourer) of fifty-five years of age, a widow, and all four sons and daughter were agricultural labourers too, the youngest of whom was James, eighteen. Everyone in the family was born at Potterne. On 5 April 1891 Ann was still there, occupying four rooms, but now she gave her age as seventy-one (according to the 1881 census this ought to have been sixty-five), and only her son Frank remained, with a granddaughter. On 2 April 1871 the census recorded that William Pearce, a general labourer, aged sixty, was domiciled at Butts, Potterne, with Ann, then forty-seven (not forty-five, as might be expected from the 1881 census, when she had been the informant), and their five children, the next to youngest of whom was James, a schoolboy of eight. They all came from Potterne, and it is likely that any surviving school admission registers there would note the various comings and goings of several generations of Pearces, and not least, their dates of birth and paternity. *Kelly's Directory of Wiltshire* for 1903, in the library on the first floor of the Family Records Centre, mentions the endowment of the elementary school at Potterne in 1831, and its rebuilding and enlargement in 1865, so the family would have attended both.

The 1863 quarterly birth indexes did not yield any James Pearce registered in Wiltshire, but there were five in 1862 and 1864, the closest geographically being that of James Pearce whose birth was registered at Devizes, two miles south of Potterne, between July and September 1862.

A page of the 1881 census index for Wiltshire, showing James Pearce, aged 18, living at Potterne.

From this census we know also that James' father William Pearce died sometime between 3 April 1871 and 3 April 1881, the date of the next enumeration, probably at Potterne, where he apparently had spent all his life. As the quarterly death indexes report ages by this period, it would be possible to trace him, using his age in 1871 (sixty) as a yardstick, though the parish registers or burial board registers relating to Potterne would be easier to search. These are held in the Wiltshire Record Office at Trowbridge. His death certificate was eventually traced through the quarterly death indexes; he was found to have died at Potterne in 1874.

Death certificate of William Pearce, 30 November 1874.

The 1861 census of Potterne, although obviously not recording James, who was apparently not born until two years later, did show William Pearce, aged fifty, Ann, forty-three, and seven older offspring, two being agricultural labourers like William and Ann, and three being at school. On the night of 30 March 1851, William described himself as 'senr' (senior), and lived at Butts, in the village. He was a widower of thirty-eight, left with a young family, William 'jnr' (junior), fifteen, a thatcher like his father, Jane, thirteen, Richard eleven and Thomas, nine. His widowed mother, Ann Pearce, aged seventy-seven, made up the household unit of three generations, taking the family's history back to her approximate birth year of 1774, at nearby Devizes. Ann was a pauper, formerly a servant, so Potterne's churchwardens' account books should reveal exactly what financial assistance she received and how often. Her son and grandchildren were all natives of Potterne, and it is possible that she came to look after the bereaved family or be supported by them herself soon after William was widowed.

William Pearce fathered at least four children before the 1851 census, by a wife as yet unknown, had remarried by 1853 when his son George was said to have been born, and then another seven children after him, whose mother was Ann. George was at school in 1861, aged eight. Although there is a ten-year gap between Thomas, eighteen, and George, aged eight, in the 1861 census, described as sons of the head of the household, on the face of it it might seem that they were children of Ann too, and it was only when the 1851 census was searched that the true situation emerged.

The ages in the 1861 census enumerator's book have been crossed through by clerks in the Registrar General's Office in London, rendering them unreadable. In such cases you can request the original books, rather than the microfilm copies of them, for inspection at the Public Record Office, Kew, though they are held off-site and take up to five days to produce.

The censuses show that the Pearces moved around in Potterne, living at Butts in 1851, Lower Street by 1861, back in Butts by 1871, then Lower Street again by 1881, where Ann Pearce, the matriarch, still lived in 1891. They were close neighbours of the Bridewells, though the Potterne Bridwell in Flood Street, Chelsea, in 1891, has not been traced back to his purported village home in any of the earlier census returns. *Kelly's Directory of Wiltshire*, 1903, in the library, reveals that the village of Potterne then consisted of two streets, the main one running north to south on the road from Devizes to Market Lavington and Salisbury. A tithe apportionment was agreed for the parish in October 1839, and the resulting map and schedule of landowners and occupiers can be examined at the Public Record Office, Kew, or in Wiltshire Record Office, at Trowbridge. The plots will show the shape and layout of each holding at the time the Pearces lived there, and whether they were owners or tenants, plus the name of their landlord. Another useful aid is the twenty-five inch Ordnance Survey map of Potterne, compiled later in the century, which can be compared with the earlier settlement, and with present visible evidence of the village streets, houses and other features.

On 6 June 1841 William Pierce (note the different spelling) was at Potterne Wick, half a mile south of the village centre, on the road to Devizes. Although ages above fifteen were supposed to be rounded down to the nearest five, these were precisely recorded, so William was then twenty-eight (placing his birth about 1813, in Wiltshire), Mary Ann, twenty-two, William, four, Hester Jane, three, and Richard, ten months (thus he was born about August or September 1840). The 1841 census does not state marital condition, relationship of people in the household to the head, nor exact birthplaces, but on the face of it it would seem that this was William, his wife and young family.

The International Genealogical Index of Wiltshire, containing entries from Potterne parish registers between 1653 and 1895, does not include any baptisms of a James Pierce or Pearce about 1863, though William Pearce was found to have married Ann Underwood there on 10 June 1851, and Mary Ann Hampton on 22 September 1834. The IGI does not embrace burials, nor does it record everything that appears in the original registers, and there may well be errors and omissions. For these reasons it is vital that the parish registers be consulted for verification and more details.

William was married by 1836 to Mary Ann, by whom he had four children (William, Hester Jane, Richard and Thomas, the last born about 1843). By 30 March 1851 he was widowed, but when his son George was born around 1853, he was married to Ann, who provided him with a further seven children, including James Pearce, born about 1863, making a total of twelve in all recorded by the census.

The parish registers of Potterne have been deposited at Wiltshire Record Office, Trowbridge, and commence in 1556; as the family seems to have been firmly entrenched there an extensive search of these and the registers of neighbouring parishes, would be worthwhile, as well as help to sort out the missing baptism, marriage and burial entries of the nineteenth century, starting with William's own about 1811 or 1813. There is a printed copy of the registers in the library of the Society of Genealogists, in London, for the years 1575-1837, so later events will have to be sought locally or among the indexes at the Family Records Centre, where you will have to purchase copies of all certificates.

Your own family tree

If you want to search the parish records of one particular area outside London, and have friends or family history contacts there, it would be cheaper to have the parish registers examined and the census microfilms, and to visit the local superintendent registrar's office, rather than make the journey to London. Alternatively you could plan a trip to a local family history centre of the Church of Jesus Christ of Latter-day Saints, paying to hire in films of each census you want, whatever the place, and of the relevant parish registers. The drawback here is that until you have seen each census in turn you do not know what to look at next, and hiring in films involves a time-lag. You can find out about local centres from the Enquiry Desk at the Family Records Centre on the first floor, and telephone the one you want to visit to find out about opening hours and facilities for searchers.

If you live in London or want to research several families in different parts of the country, then the Family Records Centre is the best possible place, because it combines the birth, marriage and death indexes of England, Wales and Scotland with census microfilms of England, Wales, the Channel Islands and Isle of Man, and those of the Scottish censuses of 1881 and 1891 in one building, accessible (except for Scotland) free of charge. From these you can then go on to explore *FamilySearch*, the vast computerised database of personal names, and the International Genealogical Index for baptisms and marriages of earlier generations, and go to the Society of Genealogists to scan any copies they may have of parish registers relevant to you (listed in *The Phillimore Atlas and Index of Parish Registers*, edited by C Humphery-Smith, 2nd ed. 1995, and in its own printed catalogue, both of which you can consult in the library on the first floor of the Family Records Centre).

The choice is yours; perhaps you may opt to search centrally housed material first, and then look at local copies to tidy up unfinished business and any loose ends, so long as you know what you are doing and plan ahead. You will probably unearth all sorts of unexpected details once you begin to delve into the history of your family. You may find forebears from different parts of the country: these two case studies, for example, show us a family leaving London to migrate down to the Sussex coast, and another coming up from rural Wiltshire, finally uniting by marriage in Brighton in 1920. They illustrate the lure of the Family Records Centre and what can be achieved with a little time and enthusiasm.

Bibliography

A selective bibliography of books mentioned in the text:

Breed G R *My Ancestors were Baptists* (SOG, 3rd ed.1995)

Camp A *My Ancestors Moved in England or Wales* (SOG, 1994)

Chapman C R *Pre-1841 Censuses and Population Listings in the British Isles* (Lochin, 1992)

Clifford D J H *My Ancestors were Congregationalists in England and Wales* (SOG, 2nd ed. 1997)

Colwell S *Dictionary of Genealogical Sources in the Public Record Office* (Weidenfeld and Nicolson, 1992)

Cox J and Padfield T *Tracing Your Ancestors in the Public Record Office* (4th ed. by Amanda Bevan and Andrea Duncan, HMSO, 1990, 5th ed. in preparation)

Cox J *New to Kew?* (PRO Publications,1997)

Fowler S, Spencer W and Tamblin S *Army Service Records of the First World War* (PRO Publications, 2nd ed. 1997)

Gibson J *Bishops' Transcripts and Marriage Licences: a Guide to their Location and Indexes* (FFHS, 4th ed. 1997)

Gibson J *Probate Jurisdictions: Where to Look for Wills* (FFHS, 4th ed.1994, updated 1997)

Gibson J and Hampson E *Marriage and Census Indexes for Family Historians* (FFHS, 7th ed. 1998)

Gibson J and Hampson E *Census Returns 1841-1891 on Microform: a directory of local holdings* (FFHS, 6th ed. 1994)

Gibson J and Peskett P *Record Offices: How to Find Them* (FFHS, 8th ed. 1998)

Gibson J and Medlycott M *Local Census Listings, 1522-1930* (FFHS, 3rd ed. 1997)

Gibson J and Rogers C *Coroners' Records in England and Wales* (FFHS, 2nd ed. 1997)

Guildhall Library Research Guide 2 *The British Overseas* (Guildhall Library, 3rd ed. revised 1995)

Guppy H B *Homes of Family Names* (London, 1890, reprinted 1968)

Humphery-Smith C R *The Phillimore Atlas and Index of Parish Registers* (Chichester, 2nd ed. 1995)

Hurley B (ed.) *The Book of Trades or Library of Useful Arts, Vols 1 and 2,1811* (Wiltshire Family History Society, 1977), *Vol 3, 1818* (Wiltshire FHS, 1994)

Johnson K A and Sainty M *Genealogical Research Directory* (Sydney, annual)

Kemp T J *International Vital Records Handbook* (Genealogical Publishing Co. Inc., Baltimore, 1994)

Leary W *My Ancestors were Methodists* (SOG, 2nd ed. reprinted 1993)

Lumas S *Making Use of the Census* (PRO Publications, 3rd ed. 1997)

Milligan E H and Thomas M J *My Ancestors were Quakers* (SOG, 1983)

Newport J A *An Index to Civil Registration Districts of England and Wales, 1837 to date* (Peter Pledger, Selsey, 1989)

Ruston A *My Ancestors were English Presbyterians/Unitarians* (SOG, 1993)

Scott M *Prerogative Court of Canterbury Wills and other Probate Records* (PRO Publications,1997)

Shorney D *Protestant Nonconformity and Roman Catholicism: a Guide to Sources in the Public Record Office* (PRO Publications, 1996)

Sinclair C *Tracing Your Scottish Ancestors* (HMSO, revised ed. 1997)

Steel D *National Index of Parish Registers,vol 2: Sources for Nonconformist Genealogy and Family History* (SOG, 1980)

Twining A and S *Dictionary of Old Trades and Occupations* (Woodcroft, Australia, 1995)